London 2012
training guide
Cycling

First published by Carlton Books Limited 2011
Copyright © 2011 Carlton Books Limited

London 2012 emblem(s) © The London Organising Committee of the Olympic
Games and Paralympic Games Ltd (LOCOG) 2007. London 2012 Pictograms
© LOCOG 2009. All rights reserved.

Carlton Books Limited,
20 Mortimer Street,
London, W1T 3JW

A CIP catalogue record for this book is available from the British Library.
10 9 8 7 6 5 4 3 2 1

ISBN: 978-1-84732-696-6

Printed in China

Editor: Matthew Lowing
Design Direction: Darren Jordan
Design: Fresh Flame
Editorial: Jo Murray and Chris Parker
Picture Research: Paul Langan
Illustrations: Glyn Walton
Production: Karin Kolbe

Tim Clifford is a lifelong cyclist, who co-founded Brixton Cycles then
embarked on a journalism career. He was launch editor of *Mountain
Biker International* and a staff writer at *Cycling Weekly*, and has
written for the *Sunday Express* and the *Sunday Times*.

London 2012
training guide

Cycling

From beginner to champion

Tim Clifford

CARLTON

Contents

Foreword by Sir Chris Hoy MBE

I have always loved riding my bike, and it is fantastic to see so many more people getting involved in cycling and participating in the sport at every level.

From an early age I enjoyed the process of setting goals and training hard to achieve them. You have to commit to a lot of hard work and make some pretty big sacrifices to achieve your goals, but it is definitely worth it.

The goal of winning another Olympic gold medal in London is what drives me on every day. Competing in a home Olympic Games is going to be an incredible experience and a once-in-a-lifetime opportunity for many of the athletes.

This *London 2012 Training Guide* will teach you the basics of the main cycling disciplines and events, as well as the importance of preparation – mental and physical – for major competitions. I hope you find this book useful as an introduction to cycling, and whether you're watching the racing or getting on a bike for the first time, have fun and enjoy it!

Sir Chris Hoy, MBE

Introduction

'Faster, Higher, Stronger' is the motto of the Olympic Games. When the world's athletes gather in London in July 2012, all will aim to live up to that ideal. Watching the sprinters flash by in the Velodrome, it is easy to forget that they share with us that moment when we rode a bike for the first time.

Cycling is for everyone. Few other forms of exercise are as much fun and can be enjoyed by toddlers and pensioners alike, with family, friends or alone. Hop on a bike and you immediately enjoy a sense of independence. Every ride is an adventure, an opportunity to explore.

It's also eco-friendly. With every turn of the pedal, you not only do your bit for the environment, but also get closer to nature. You become part of the landscape, aware of the ground beneath your wheels and of the changing seasons.

You don't have to be fit to start cycling, yet will quickly come to appreciate its health benefits. The British Heart Foundation estimates that riding just 20 miles (32 kilometres) a week can halve the risk of heart disease, the UK's biggest killer, because cycling strengthens the heart, lungs and cardiovascular system.

What's more, regularly riding a bike makes you look and feel younger. It reduces the risk of cancer and diabetes, boosts the immune system, encourages weight loss, reduces stress, improves sleep patterns, tones muscles and improves strength and flexibility, making everyday tasks easier. Unlike running, it doesn't put undue stress on the joints, making it a particularly suitable form of exercise for older people.

The true genius of the bicycle is that it offers all these benefits while also being a form of transport. Commuting to work, school or college by bike fits healthy exercise into the daily routine. The money saved on petrol or public transport will soon recoup the cost of even the most expensive bike.

Making the same journey every day will improve your health and fitness. But your body will quickly grow used to this level of exercise and your speed and stamina will reach a plateau and stop improving. To take them to the next level, you need to understand how to cycle faster and how to cover greater distances.

Showing you how to do this is one aim of this book. Another is to explain competitive cycling's many disciplines and encourage you to have a go at them. Here we run up against one facet of the sport many newcomers find daunting: technology. Bikes are machines subject to constant refinement as manufacturers strive to produce higher, faster, stronger bikes, too.

It's the rider, not the bike, however, that wins races. You do not need an expensive, state-of-the-art bike to start competing. On road or off, against yourself or against others, in events that last seconds or hours, bike racing is fun, sociable and open to people of all ages and abilities.

Be inspired by the world's best riders as they do battle in London. Then go out and discover the kind of cycling that suits you best. Once you find it, you will relish the freedom that comes with riding a bike, make friends, enjoy a sense of fulfilment and, who knows, there might even be a place for you on the podium at a future Olympic Games. After all, every Olympic victory starts with a dream.

Britain's success at the 2008 Olympic Games has helped revive cycling's popularity.

The basics

The rider is the engine of any bike, so successful cyclists take care of both their health and their equipment. Their training is tailored to their chosen branch of the sport and their bikes are designed and engineered for it.

Cycling at the Olympic Games

At the London 2012 Games cyclists will compete for medals in four disciplines – Track, Road, Mountain Bike and BMX. The first two have long histories while cross-country Mountain Biking was introduced at the Atlanta 1996 Games and BMX made its debut at Beijing 2008.

The Discipline: Track Cycling

Men and women will both contest five events on the 250-metre wooden track in London's new Velodrome. Rule changes since Beijing 2008 mean nations can field only one entry – individual or team – per event, so there will be no repeat of Britain's multiple medal haul of 2008.

Track Cycling is divided into two broad categories: sprint events of between three and eight laps, where success often depends on raw power; and endurance events, which are much longer and require great stamina and tactical awareness.

The sprint events at the Olympic Games are the Sprint, Team Sprint, Keirin and, as part of the Omnium, the 250m flying start Time Trial and the 1km Time Trial. The endurance events are the Team Pursuit and the Omnium, which is comprised of the scratch race, individual pursuit, points race and elimination race.

Sprint

The basics: a series of three-lap races between two riders with only the last 200m timed. Riders go head to head in the best of three races to determine progress in each round. The usual winning strategy in a race is to let an opponent lead the way, then accelerate to the front just before the finish line, leaving

them with no opportunity to respond.

Because nobody wants to take the lead, the first two laps are a tactical game of cat and mouse, often ridden at slow speed. When battle commences, the action is fast and furious.

What it takes to win: sprinters work hard on strength training in the gym to build the powerful muscles needed for explosive but short-lived turns of speed. Intense concentration is also required to avoid being caught out by sudden attacks.

Team Sprint

The basics: in the men's event, two teams of three riders start on opposite sides of the track and chase each other round it. At the end of lap one, the first rider in each team peels off up the banking, followed at the end of lap two by the second rider, leaving the third man to complete the final lap alone. The women's event follows the same format, but is contested by two-rider teams racing over two laps.

What it takes to win: the ability to accelerate quickly and maintain a high-intensity effort over a short time are key ingredients, as is teamwork and disciplined riding technique. Riding in the slipstream of another rider requires less energy as the lead rider is battling against wind resistance, so the second and third riders must know exactly when to accelerate so that they are travelling at full speed at the moment when the lead rider peels off.

Keirin

The basics: an eight-lap race contested by up to eight riders, who draft behind a pacing motorcycle, known as a Derny, for the first five and a half laps. The Derny gradually increases speed from 30 kilometres per hour up to about 50km per hour (25–45km per hour for women). When the Derny pulls off the track, the riders race each other for the final 600–700 metres.

What it takes to win: Keirin riders share a lot in common with sprint specialists. Both disciplines demand speed and tactical awareness. Physical presence helps, too, because there is a lot of jockeying for position behind the Derny.

Team Pursuit

The basics: two teams start on opposite sides of the track and chase each other around it. Men compete in teams of four over 16 laps (4km), women in teams of three over 12 laps (3km). Riders share the pace-making, taking turns at the front before swinging up the banking, then rejoining the back of the line. The object is to cover the distance in the fastest time – recorded on the time of the third rider across the line – or to catch the other team.

What it takes to win: great endurance with an ability to ride at high intensity over four minutes. Very precise riding skills are required, too, as making a smooth transition from riding at the front of the group to the back is critical to success.

Successful Track cyclists require good speed and tactical awareness.

The Omnium

The basics: an Omnium comprises a series of six races in which contestants compete against each other. They are:

1. 250m flying lap: competitors are allowed two or three laps of the track to get up to top speed before the clock starts on their run.

2. Points race (30km for men and 20km for women): riders compete for points awarded for sprints that take place every 10 laps. The first rider across the finishing line in each sprint wins five points, the second three, the third two, and the fourth one. Riders can also attempt to lap the field at any time, a manoeuvre that earns them 20 points.

3. Elimination race: every other lap is a sprint, with the last rider across the line eliminated from the race.

4. Individual pursuit (4km for men and 3km for women): riders start from opposite sides of the track and are awarded points for their time.

5. Scratch race (15km for men and 10km for women): entails a massed start and fast racing from the off.

6. Time trial (1km for men and 500m for women): riders aim to post the fastest time over the set distance.

What it takes to win: a rider has to be good at sprinting, time trialling and bunched racing.

The Discipline: Road Cycling

In the Olympic Games there are two events that take place on the road. One is the mass-start Road Race and the other the Time Trial, where each competitor races alone against the clock.

Road Race cycling requires excellent bike-handling skills on account of the number of competitors.

Road Race

The basics: riders start together, then race along a closed circuit of roads with the first past the line declared the winner. The one-day Road Races at Beijing 2008 were 245km for men and 126.4km for women and the London 2012 routes are expected to cover similar distances.

What it takes to win: to be competitive in an event that lasts more than six hours and doesn't slow down for stragglers requires great stamina, tactical awareness and teamwork. If the race ends in a sprint, controlled aggression, hidden reserves of energy and supportive team-mates all come into play.

Time Trial

The basics: known for good reason as 'the race of truth', the Time Trial is competitive cycling in its purest form: individual riders set off at identical intervals, usually a minute apart, and race against the clock over a set distance on tarmac. Whoever records the fastest time is the winner. The London 2012 course has yet to be finalised. At Beijing 2008, men rode a 47.3km time trial and women a 23.8km one.

What it takes to win: great endurance and the ability to maintain a high speed for a long time. Successful competitors know themselves well and know how to pace their effort so they don't go too fast too soon and run out of energy, or too slow that they lose time to their rivals.

The Discipline: Mountain Bike Cross-country

The basics: a massed-start race across varied terrain that includes significant amounts of climbing and descending, with the first across the finish line the winner. Courses are typically a mix of forest tracks, unpaved roads, dirt patches and fields. At Beijing 2008, the men raced eight laps of a 4.5km circuit, 36km in total, and the women six laps, 27km in total.

The Discipline: BMX

The basics: first-past-the-post racing in which eight riders start from a platform, usually 8m high. When the gate drops, they speed down an incline on to a purpose-built 300–400m-long dirt track full of bumps, tabletops, banked corners and straight sections. Initially, riders compete in heats – known as motos

Mountain bike courses are designed to test every aspect of riders' bike-handling skills.

BMX, which stands for Bicycle Moto Cross, made its Olympic debut in Beijing 2008.

– of three races, with the four most consistently successful competitors in each heat progressing to the next round until just eight riders are left to contest the Olympic final, a single race that decides the medals.

What it takes to win: sprinting from the word go requires explosive power. Riders compete shoulder to shoulder, negotiate multiple obstacles and are often airborne, so excellent bike handling skills and plenty of nerve are needed too. Less well recognised are the need for a good tactical brain – aware of both the best line to ride and the opposition – and the ability to recover quickly. In the course of a meet, racers compete often and have to be at their best each time to avoid elimination.

Getting started

Perhaps the Olympic Games have inspired you to take up cycling or maybe you want to get fit and shed a few pounds. First, be honest with yourself about the state of your health, then decide what sort of cycling you want to do and start looking for your first serious bike.

The Cost

Confronted with a vast choice of bikes ranging in price from one hundred pounds to thousands of pounds, it is easy to forget that cycling is a combination of man and machine. Expensive equipment is seductive, but fitness and experience win races. A good entry-level bike does not have to break the bank. The starting point for decent-quality bikes suitable for competition is £250 for a BMX and £400–£500 for road and mountain bikes. What matters most is that it is the right size for you (see pages 38–9).

Which Bike?

The first step is to be clear in your mind about how you intend to use the bike. Don't be tempted to specialise too quickly. Riding a time trial bike, for instance, is daunting for a beginner

Shopping for a bike

- Buy from a specialist bike shop, with staff who know their products and are expert at matching customers to bikes. Ideally, bikes will have been assembled by an experienced mechanic and receive a free first service.
- Be clear about the type of riding you want to do and how much you want to spend. Ask about the quality of the ride, frame sizing, frame materials and components of the bikes on offer and for explanations of any jargon you don't understand.
- Test-ride bikes at the top and bottom end of your price range to see how they compare – a good bike shop will let you do this, but be prepared to pay a deposit and leave ID. Ask the salesperson to check your riding position and recommend any necessary changes. A good shop will willingly make adjustments and even swap components to ensure correct fit.
- Look out for sales – manufacturers introduce new models annually and in late summer and autumn many shops sell off last year's models at a discount.
- Buying secondhand is another option, but be careful – unwary buyers may be sold stolen or damaged bikes and will only realise when parts fail and they are on their way to A&E.

Health check

Cycling, like any form of exercise, puts stress on the body that is potentially dangerous to anyone unused to it. Before going to the expense of buying a bike, if you are over the age of 40 and have not exercised regularly or have a family history of heart disease, strokes or sudden death at an early age ask your doctor for a health check. A doctor will assess your lifestyle and medical history, and may measure your blood pressure, take a blood sample to check cholesterol levels and possibly recommend an electrocardiogram (ECG) test. Once you receive the all-clear and begin to ride, be realistic and start slowly. Attempt too much too soon and you may not only put your health at risk but also lose your enthusiasm for riding a bike.

because it is less stable than a road bike. Freestyle BMXs are more robust than BMX race bikes, making them more suitable for a learner keen to master bunny-hops and jumps.

Do Your Research

Surf the internet, read manufacturers' catalogues and bike magazine reviews, talk to friends about their bikes and, if you can, ride as many bikes as possible to see how they feel. Visit your local bike shop, too, and ask their advice.

Before you get on a bike, consider having a fitness assessment to ensure you are fit to ride.

Cycling clubs

If you are serious about taking up cycling, a wise first step is to join a club. Club membership gives you access to training advice from coaches and experienced riders, regular club rides and a wider range of competitive options, as well as providing fun, social events.

Join Up!

Whatever your age or branch of cycling, it is strongly advisable to join a club. British Cycling has developed the Go-Ride scheme for under-16s to introduce them to all branches of the sport. Go-Ride-accredited clubs have qualified coaches to teach skills to under-16s in a safe environment away from public roads.

For under-12s, the emphasis is on having fun, with specialist coaches encouraging young people to try different cycling activities and to develop their confidence and bike handling ability through games. For 12–16-year-olds, the principles of training are gradually introduced, so that by the age of 16 they should have a good understanding of how to train properly. Go-Ride Racing, the scheme's newest initiative, aims to encourage more young people into entry-level racing.

For older riders new to the sport, club membership also has much to offer, from fun rides and social events to help at races and contact with coaches who can offer objective advice on how to build on your strengths and improve on

your weaknesses. Before you seek out a coach's help, spend some time thinking about what you want to achieve (see pages 56–7).

Cycling clubs are not only fun environments but they are also places to develop your skills.

You can find details of clubs in your area through British Cycling's website, britishcycling.org.uk.

British Cycling Membership

To race in Track, Road Racing, Mountain Bike and BMX events, you need to be a member of British Cycling, the sport's governing body, which offers a variety of membership packages from under-12s to adult. These provide benefits such as accident insurance, access to coaching, newsletters and racing calendars. Basic packages come with a provisional racing licence, which allows you to race in entry-level events.

Beyond that level, you will need a full racing licence, which is free for under-16s but costs extra for juniors (16–18) and adults. With a full racing licence you can collect points based on your race results that allow you to move up from one category to the next. A full explanation of the ranking and category system can be found on the British Cycling website.

Cycling Time Trials

Time trialling is organised by Cycling Time Trials (CTT), not British Cycling, so if you are interested in this branch of the sport, it is worth joining a CTT-affiliated club. Many clubs run 'Come and Try It' events – all you have to do is turn up on the day, pay a nominal £2–£3 entry fee and ride. To take part in competitive time trialling you will also need to be a member of a CTT-affiliated club. To find your nearest club, visit the CTT website, cyclingtimetrials.org.uk.

The bike

The bicycle is a supremely efficient machine for turning human energy into motion, the equivalent of a car getting 3,000 miles per gallon of petrol. That hasn't stopped its evolution. People are constantly thinking of new ways to make it even better.

The bicycle — a brief history

Travel is such an accepted part of our lives that it is easy to forget that two centuries ago people were dependent on animals or their own two feet to get from A to B.

The Running Machine

The dream of a human-powered vehicle to speed up journeys was first realised by Baron Karl von Drais, a German inventor. In 1817 he built a 'running machine' – a wooden frame, with two iron-rimmed wooden wheels and a handlebar to steer the front wheel. Sitting astride it and scooting along with his feet, von Drais was able to travel for long periods and, when going downhill, take his feet off the ground without falling over. That simple act of balancing began the bicycle's evolution. Von Drais took his invention to Paris where the Draisienne, or velocipede as the French called it, became a fad that spread to England and America. But with the advent of the first railways the velocipede faded from view for more than 40 years.

Pedal Power

In 1864 a French invention – the attachment of pedals to the front wheel – brought it back into fashion. Who came up with the idea is disputed. The father and son team of Pierre and Ernest Michaux have their advocates, while Pierre Lallement, who emigrated to America where he filed a patent for a front-wheel drive bike in 1866, is the other main contender. The novelty of travelling on two wheels sent velocipede

Significant bike: The Rover Safety

At the Stanley Show in London in 1885, John Kemp Starley and his business partner William Sutton unveiled the machine that would shape cycling's future: the Rover Safety. Although the first frames did not have a seat tube, the design shares many characteristics with the modern bike: a diamond-shaped frame with a forward-sloping head tube, wheels of similar size, and pedals mounted at the bottom bracket, powering the rear wheel by chain, rather than attached to the front wheel. Suddenly the high-wheeler was obsolete as the Rover took the world by storm and other manufacturers rushed to imitate it.

It wasn't long after the invention of the bicycle was invented that people began to race them.

mania sweeping through France, America and Britain. Bike manufacturers built machines first of cast iron and then of wrought iron, schools sprang up to teach people how to ride and, in 1868, the first bicycle race was held in Paris.

The Penny-farthing

By 1870 the craze was over, halted in France by war with Prussia and in America by the poor state of the roads, although in Britain the decline was less pronounced. That year saw the introduction of the Ordinary or penny-farthing. Built for speed, these had massive front wheels of up to 60 inches (1.5 metres) in diameter and small rear wheels averaging 17 inches (43 centimetres).

Technical Developments

At first glance, the penny-farthing looks like an evolutionary dead end as far as bicycle design goes, but it helped refine innovations such as wire-spoked tensionable wheels, patented by the Frenchman Eugene Meyer in 1869. James Starley, father of the British cycle industry, patented tangentially spoked wheels in 1874 and they are still in use today. While Meyer was the first man to build a penny-farthing, Starley's Ariel high wheelers were the first to be produced in quantity. Other changes were afoot too. Solid rubber tyres replaced iron hoops, hollow steel frames overtook wrought-iron ones and the introduction of ball bearings made wheel rotation and steering smoother.

Safety Concerns

By the mid-1870s there were an estimated 50,000 high wheelers in Britain, but riding them was dangerous. A new approach was needed. In 1879, Henry Lawson, an English manufacturer, produced the Bicyclette, the first bike with a chain-driven rear wheel. The design was a commercial failure, but the chain drive was not forgotten. In 1884, the first safety bicycles appeared in Britain. The most famous of these was the Rover Safety, introduced the following year by John Kemp Starley, nephew of James Starley, and it was quickly copied by other manufacturers.

A Comfortable Ride

Riding a bike, even after the developments of the 1870s and 1880s, was still uncomfortable. In 1888, John Boyd Dunlop, a Scots vet working in Belfast, began experimenting with air-filled tyres, which led him and his business partner Harvey du Cros to set up the Dunlop Pneumatic Tyre Company in Dublin. When Harvey's son, Arthur, came to London in 1889 to demonstrate the firm's tyres, he was laughed at in the streets. But the new tyres made cycling comfortable and contributed to a massive boom in its popularity in the 1890s.

Boom Years

Because bikes were expensive, they first caught on with the affluent. Members of high society went to gymnasiums to learn to ride, then met in Battersea and Hyde Parks to parade their skills. For the first time, cycling was accessible to women, too, and it was taken up by famous figures such as the actresses Ellen Terry and Lillie Langtry. Racing became popular, both on the track and in long-distance races such as Paris–Roubaix, first held in 1896. Competition between

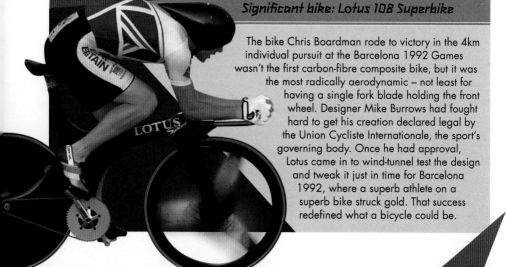

Significant bike: Lotus 108 Superbike

The bike Chris Boardman rode to victory in the 4km individual pursuit at the Barcelona 1992 Games wasn't the first carbon-fibre composite bike, but it was the most radically aerodynamic – not least for having a single fork blade holding the front wheel. Designer Mike Burrows had fought hard to get his creation declared legal by the Union Cycliste Internationale, the sport's governing body. Once he had approval, Lotus came in to wind-tunnel test the design and tweak it just in time for Barcelona 1992, where a superb athlete on a superb bike struck gold. That success redefined what a bicycle could be.

manufacturers brought prices down, making bikes affordable for ordinary people and heralding a social revolution. Mobility broadened the horizons of men and women of all classes.

The invention of the car inevitably dented the bicycle's popularity, but it didn't kill it off. Cycle racing – the first Tour de France took place in 1903 – and cycle tourism thrived in Europe, and in countries such as Holland the bicycle became a staple form of transport. The pace of change for the bicycle itself slowed, although refinements such as multiple gears were introduced.

Recent Developments

Concern for the environment and an appreciation of cycling's health benefits led to a resurgence in its popularity in the 1960s, but it was the arrival of BMX and mountain biking in the 1960s and 1970s

that made cycling cool. The boom has prompted a wave of development. Frame materials such as titanium, aluminium and carbon-fibre composite have been introduced and refined. Indexed shifting has simplified gear changing and put it at the riders' fingertips. Suspension systems have encouraged people to venture off-road. Today's bikes have come a long way since the Draisienne, but the independence they provide is just the same.

Modern bicycles are light and aerodynamic and often made of advanced materials such as aluminium, titanium or carbon-fibre composites.

The modern bike

The majority of bikes are purchased simply to get about. Competitive cycling, though, demands performance. Specialist machines are created to suit the demands of each discipline.

The Frame

The frame is at the heart of every bicycle. What sets one bike apart from another are the materials used in its frame construction, the dimensions and angles chosen when those materials are joined together and the components fitted to the finished frame.

Carbon fibre: in track and road racing, weight and aerodynamics matter greatly, so the most expensive frames are made of carbon-fibre composite. Originally developed in the aerospace industry, carbon-fibre composite can be moulded into any shape, giving strength and stiffness where needed. It is also good

at absorbing high-frequency vibrations, which is why many metal bikes have carbon-fibre composite fork blades.

Titanium: this is light and rustproof but not as stiff as carbon-fibre composite. Oversized tubing gets around this problem, but it is an expensive raw material and can only be welded in oxygen-free conditions, which adds to the cost, so very few frames are made from it.

Aluminium: aluminium alloy has overtaken steel as the most widely used frame material because of its better strength to weight ratio. Advances in alloying, heat treatment and in the

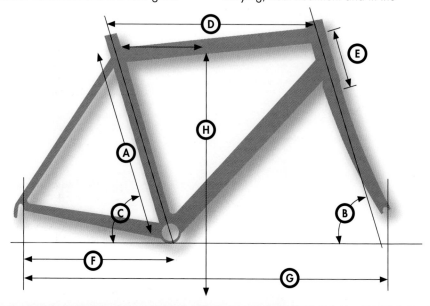

production of oversized and butted tubing have led to durable frames often noticeably stiffer than steel ones.

Steel: this is heavier than aluminium and prone to rust but it is very strong, cheap and produces a comfortable ride. Frames made of it are now found at opposite ends of the spectrum – cheap, heavy bikes are made of hi-tensile steel, an alloy of iron and carbon, and high-quality bikes are made of chromoly steel, an alloy of iron, chrome and molybdenum. Because of steel's durability, good chromoly steel bikes suitable for racing can easily be found on the second-hand market.

Frame geometry

The length of the frame tubes and the angles at which they are joined affect the fit of the bike and the way it handles. Broadly, steeper head tube and seat tube angles produce a faster but less comfortable ride, fine for the track or a time trial but unforgiving over distance. The handling, too, is less stable.

Every manufacturer's catalogue contains details about frame geometry. It is useful to know what these mean, though they don't tell the whole story. Tyre pressure and saddle position affect handling, too, so going for a ride gives a better understanding of how a bike behaves.

A. Seat tube length: from centre of the bottom bracket to centre of the top tube, or centre of the bottom bracket to top of the seat tube, this was the traditional measurement for sizing a bike until the advent of sloping top tubes reduced its importance.

B. Head tube angle: formed by a line through the centre of the head tube and the ground. Fork rake, the distance the front axle is set forward from this line, also affects steering.

C. Seat tube angle: formed by a line through the centre of the seat tube and the ground. Frame size affects this measurement but it is also adjusted to move a rider's centre of gravity in relation to the pedals, with a steeper angle producing a less comfortable ride.

D. Top tube length: distance along a notional horizontal line from the centre of the head tube to the centre of the seatpost on sloping tube bikes. Used by many manufacturers as the key measurement in bike fit. If the top tube is parallel to the ground, it is measured from centre of the head tube to centre of the seatpost.

E. Head tube: a measurement largely dictated by frame size.

F. Chainstay length: from centre of the bottom bracket to centre of the rear axle. Shorter chainstays improve acceleration and manoeuvrability; longer ones improve comfort and stability.

G. Wheelbase: from the centre of the front and rear axles. A shorter wheelbase produces a livelier, less stable ride.

H. Standover height: measured from centre of the top tube to the ground. If you can't stand over the bike with your feet flat on the ground, you risk a painful whack in the groin when you come to a stop.

Anatomy of a track bike

Track bikes can be the simplest or the most sophisticated type of bike. On the one hand, the stripped-down bikes visible at every track meeting; on the other, the highly specialised aerodynamic bikes used by elite riders in events such as the one kilometre time trial and team pursuit.

Basic Anatomy

Desirable qualities: a light, stiff frame that quickly transfers as much rider power as possible into forward motion.

Frame materials: aluminium, carbon-fibre composite and chromoly steel are the most popular choices. The bike shown is made of oversized aluminium alloy tubing that is butted, so the tubes' internal walls are thicker at points of stress, principally the joints, and thinner elsewhere. Oversizing improves rigidity and power transmission. The forks have carbon-fibre composite blades and an aluminum alloy steering tube, a combination that adds a bit of comfort.

Tyres: very narrow, 19–22 millimetres wide, with no or very little tread pattern, and pumped up hard to reduce rolling resistance. The track is also one of the few places where tubular tyres, which glue to the rim, haven't been entirely replaced by wired-on clinchers.

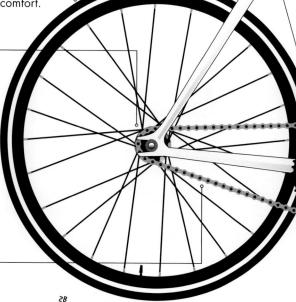

Gears: single-speed.

Drivetrain: the chainset has a single chainring at the front that drives a fixed rear sprocket. The number of teeth on both determines how far the bike travels with every pedal revolution. A large number of teeth on the chainring combined with a small number of teeth on the sprocket will produce very high speeds but require more rider energy to turn the pedals.

Guided Tour

Frame features: a higher bottom bracket, which increases pedal clearance on the banking but also affects stability. A short wheelbase and steep head and seat tube angles enhance power transmission at the expense of comfort.

Short chainstays bring the rear wheel close to the seat tube. The rear dropouts – the slots for the rear wheel – face backward. This allows the wheel to be moved back to tension the chain.

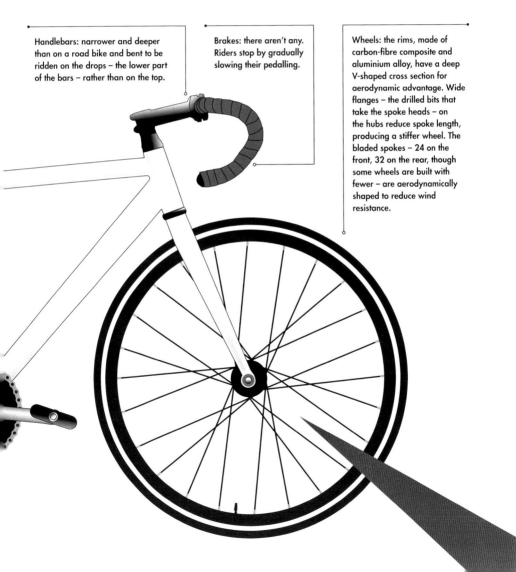

Handlebars: narrower and deeper than on a road bike and bent to be ridden on the drops – the lower part of the bars – rather than on the top.

Brakes: there aren't any. Riders stop by gradually slowing their pedalling.

Wheels: the rims, made of carbon-fibre composite and aluminium alloy, have a deep V-shaped cross section for aerodynamic advantage. Wide flanges – the drilled bits that take the spoke heads – on the hubs reduce spoke length, producing a stiffer wheel. The bladed spokes – 24 on the front, 32 on the rear, though some wheels are built with fewer – are aerodynamically shaped to reduce wind resistance.

Anatomy of a road bike

An ideal entry point for newcomers to the sport, a road bike is suitable for both the road race and time trials. For amateur and professional alike, it must be both a workhorse and a powerhouse, able to be ridden for hours without discomfort but still deliver the goods in a sprint finish.

Basic Anatomy

Desirable qualities: a good strength to weight ratio and a frame that is responsive yet forgiving enough for long hours in the saddle.

Frame materials: aluminium has replaced chromoly steel as the most commonly-used frame material, followed by carbon-fibre composite and, more rarely, titanium. This entry-level road bike is made of butted oversized aluminium tubing and features a sloping, curved top tube. The forks have carbon-fibre composite blades that overcome the harsh ride characteristic of early aluminium bikes.

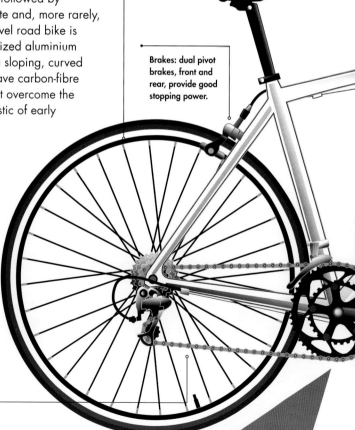

Wheels: the road bike sized wheels (commonly known as 700c) are double walled for added strength and rigidity, and the hubs have quick release levers that allow the wheels to be taken off quickly without tools. Both front and rear wheels are laced with 32 stainless-steel spokes though lots of other spoke number combinations are also available.

Brakes: dual pivot brakes, front and rear, provide good stopping power.

Drivetrain: 18 gears, supplied by two chainrings on the chainset and a nine-sprocket cassette on the rear hub. The range of gears is wide enough to maintain a steady pedalling rate, or cadence, over different types of terrain. The front and rear derailleurs move the chain from one chainring to another and from one sprocket to another when the gear levers are pulled.

Guided Tour

Frame features: the head tube and seat tube angles are more relaxed than on a track bike, and the wheelbase and chainstays are longer, too. The barely noticeable extra couple of centimetres in overall length contribute to ride comfort.

Groupsets

Most manufacturers buy the main components for their bikes from a single source, and different manufacturers produce groupsets at different price points. Components in a groupset usually include the bike's brake/gear levers, brakes, front and rear derailleurs, chainset, bottom bracket, chain and rear casette (the sprockets on the rear wheel).

Handlebar stem: this bike's stem contains a shim that allows it to be set at four different angles, an aid in fine-tuning rider position.

Brake/gear levers: one unit operates both. Pull the main levers backward to brake; flick them inward to switch gears in one direction; flick the smaller lever on the unit to switch gears in the other direction.

Handlebars: offer three positions for the hands: on the drops, on the brake levers or on the top.

Tyres: narrow 23mm tyres with a light tread are fine for racing, though many riders prefer wider tyres for day-to-day riding.

Anatomy of a time trial bike

Aerodynamics, weight and power transmission are the prime concerns of the time triallist. Out on the road alone with the clock ticking, every turn of the pedal counts and in a race against time nobody wants to feel that wind resistance has stopped them from producing a great ride.

Basic Anatomy

Desirable qualities: a light, stiff frame that quickly transfers as much rider power as possible into forward motion.

Frame materials: the top-end choice is carbon-fibre composite, while the more affordable option is aluminium alloy, ideally paired with carbon-fibre composite forks. You still see plenty of time triallists on hand-built chromoly steel bikes.

Gears: 20-speed, with two front chainrings of 53 teeth and 39 teeth, and a rear 10-speed cassette block with 11–23 teeth.

Drivetrain: an electronic shifting system not only allows precise gear shifting at the press of a button but it also self-trims. The front derailleur detects where the chain is and repositions itself to always be in place for a smooth shift.

Frame features: this is a state-of-the-art bike as ridden by Olympic and professional riders. The frame, handlebars and seatpost are all made of carbon-fibre composite aerodynamically shaped to reduce drag. The bottom bracket shell and the chainstay on the drivetrain side have been beefed up to reduce flex.

The seat tube is recessed to bring the rear wheel forward, shortening the chainstays and improving the transfer of power from the cranks to the rear wheel.

The integrated fork, handlebar and stem setup is complicated. The stem is in two aerodynamically shaped parts. The lower section attaches to the fork crown and the bars are clamped between it and the stem's upper section. To reduce drag, riders spend most of their time with their hands and arms on the extensions above this unit. These can be adjusted for height, width, length and angle.

Frame geometry is 73 degrees for the head tube angle and 78 degrees for the seat tube angle, though this can be adjusted from 74 degrees to 78 degrees by moving the saddle position on the seatpost. The ultra-short chainstays shorten the wheelbase, making for a lively ride.

Brakes: mounted behind the front fork and below the rear chainstays to reduce drag. All cables run inside the frame, also for aerodynamic reasons.

Wheels: the carbon-fibre composite and aluminium alloy rims have a very deep-section aerodynamic shape with a dimpled surface to further reduce drag. A carbon-fibre composite disc wheel is an option at the rear, provided the wind isn't blowing. The state-of-the-art hubs allow the load on the bearings to be adjusted after the quick release skewer has been tightened. Oval-shaped spokes reduce drag. The front wheel has 16 radial spokes; the back 20 spokes, built with them crossed on the non-drive side and radial on the drive side. The tyres are 700x20c tubulars, glued to the rim, with no tread.

Anatomy of a mountain bike

Narrow, twisting trails, helter-skelter descents, grinding climbs, jumps and, on a bad day, thick, thick mud: cross-country Mountain Biking embraces them all. It takes a special breed of bike to not only survive in such conditions but also excel in them.

Basic Anatomy

Desirable qualities: a strong frame is essential in a bike that has to take anything that's thrown at it, so mountain bikes weigh more than most other bikes. They also need to be very manoeuvrable and forgiving.

Frame materials: made from aluminium because of its strength to weight ratio, this bike has butted tubing to increase strength at the joints. High-end carbon-fibre composite and titanium bikes are also available. Chromoly steel still has its advocates because it is strong yet slightly flexible.

Brakes: disc brakes clamp the brake pads on to a rotor attached to the hub rather than on to the rim, which produces excellent braking power in all conditions. Better-quality setups, such as this one, are hydraulic rather than cable-operated and feature sealed tubes filled with brake fluid to push the brake pads on to the rotor.

Drivetrain: a wider and lower range of gears than on a road bike helps riders tame the terrain. This bike has a triple chainset with 44/32/22-tooth chainrings and nine rear sprockets with 11–32 teeth. The rear derailleur has a long cage to accommodate the chain's travel to the biggest sprockets.

Guided Tour

Frame features: for comfort and control, mountain bikes have more relaxed head tube and seat tube angles than road bikes. Chainstays are kept short for extra agility and, on climbs, traction. Wide clearances around the wheels prevent mud clogging.

Mountain bikes were the first to adopt the sloping top tube and long seatpost combination now found on road bikes. The smaller main triangle gives greater strength and rigidity, and allows the rider to shift body weight more easily, aiding control and traction. Suspension forks at the front absorb bumps, reducing vibrations to the hands and arms.

Handlebars: wider than on a road bike for greater control.

Gear levers: indexed shifters are mounted underneath the brake levers, so always to hand, with the levers operated by thumb and forefinger to change gear.

Suspension forks: in this piece of motocycle technology adapted for bikes, how far the inner fork leg slides within the outer fork leg is governed by a compressed air spring. An oil-filled damper, which forces the fluid through small holes from one chamber to another, controls the rebound. A knob is turned to make the forks more or less shock-absorbent depending on the terrain.

Wheels: standard wheel size is 26in. Rims are usually double walled and wide to accommodate fat tyres. Hubs are often beefed up compared to road race bikes, especially the rear one which holds the freewheel cassette for the back sprockets. The spokes for both wheels are made of thicker-gauge steel. Tyres have knobbles to provide traction on loose surfaces.

Pedals: clipless pedals are the norm for cross-country racing.

Anatomy of a BMX bike

Fast and furious, BMX racing was an instant hit when it was introduced at the Beijing 2008 Olympic Games. Elite-level athletes race on specialist machines, though the joy of BMX is that you can start racing at a local track on the same bike you use for riding around the streets.

Basic Anatomy

Desirable qualities: a race bike has to be strong enough to withstand repeated impacts from jumping yet light enough to be competitive.

Frame materials: the two main choices are aluminium, as used on this bike, and chromoly steel, particularly 4130 tubing, which has an excellent strength to weight ratio. Some racing forks now have carbon-fibre composite blades. Complete frames of the material are rare, as are titanium frames, largely because they are so expensive.

Tyres: a wider 20x1.95in tyre is fitted for greater traction and control at the front end, important when cornering at speed, and a 20.175in tyre at the back. Both have a knobbly tread pattern for riding on dirt.

Cranks or crank arms: the levers that connect the pedals to the axle inside the bottom bracket.

Gears: single-speed with a single 44-tooth chainring at the front connected to a 16-tooth sprocket attached to a cassette rear hub.

Chainset: three-piece chainsets are standard on all but the cheapest bikes, where the axle and crank arms are formed from a single piece of metal.

Pedals: experienced racers will use clipless pedals, although most bikes come with double-sided platform pedals that provide some grip for shoes.

Guided Tour

Frame features: a 71-degree seat tube angle and 73-degree head tube angle are standard geometry for most BMXs. Chainstays on a race bike are longer than on freestyle bikes, partly to ensure the bike's front end doesn't pop up when the rider starts pedalling as the gate drops and partly for greater stability. Bottom bracket height is lower on a race bike to enhance power transmission.

Handlebars: upright bars formed from two pieces of welded chromoly steel, one a cross-brace to increase rigidity. The ends of the bars are angled back and slightly upward. One rule of racing is that the handlebar grips must cover the ends of the bars to reduce the risks of injury in an accident.

Brakes: a single linear pull V-brake mounted on the seatstays, used for control more than stopping.

Extras: for racing, bikes must be equipped with padding on the top tube, stem and handlebar cross-brace.

Wheels: 20in diameter wheels are the norm. These have to be strong, so rims are usually double or triple walled internally. Both wheels are laced with 32 spokes on this race bike, though 36-spoke wheels are common on freestyle bikes. The gauge of the spokes is thicker than on a road bike. This bike has sealed bearing hubs, with lightweight hollow axles.

Bottom bracket set: this bike has a sealed bearing unit with hollow chromoly axles. It is worth asking about the bottom bracket when buying a bike as BMX bottom brackets come in four types, which can lead to compatibility problems when changing components.

Bike fit and setup

A dream bike can prove to be a nightmare ride if it isn't the right size, taking the fun out of cycling and replacing it with aches and pains. For maximum comfort and control, make sure that you and your bike are a perfect fit.

People come in so many shapes and sizes and achieving correct bike position involves so many variables that it's easy to understand why bike fitting services are big business in the United States and becoming increasingly popular in the UK.

Manufacturers don't make life easier by measuring their bikes in different ways. One firm's 17in mountain bike may be quite unlike a rival's firm's bike of nominally the same size.

What matters most in the end is that the bike fits you rather than you trying to fit the bike. A good bike shop will make sure this is the case and test riding a selection of bikes will confirm it for you. The bike has to feel right.

The information in this section is for bikes with 700c (road bike wheels) or 26in wheels) (the size of most mountain bike wheels. It assumes long hours in the saddle rather than short bursts on the track where riders want power and aerodynamic advantage more than comfort.

Riding Position Basics
Head: upright so the eyes can scan ahead as far as possible, letting you choose the best line to ride early.
Arms: sloping forward with elbows slightly bent. If they take too much weight, they will become tired and ache.
Hands: relaxed yet firm and in control, thumbs hooked around the bars, fingers in easy reach of the gear and brake levers.
Torso/shoulders: a body rocking from side to side wastes energy, it should be

still, not overstretched, and the shoulders relaxed to avoid back and neck pain.
Handlebars: shoulder width or wider to avoid restricted breathing. Setting the handlebar height depends on back flexibility and the type of riding you do.
Saddle: keep it level, so it's in contact with the same sit bones you feel sitting on a bench.
Feet: for starters, keep them horizontal with the ball of the foot above the pedal axle.
Knees: slightly bent when the pedal is at the bottom of the down stroke.

Bike Fit

Frame size and bike fit are not the same thing. The advent of sloping top tube and compact geometries has complicated bike sizing, and some manufacturers now simply label their frames like T-shirts as small, medium, large and extra large.

You can estimate frame size by measuring your inside leg from crotch to

Track bikes are designed for aerodynamic efficiency rather than comfort.

floor in stocking feet, then subtract 10in for a road bike or 12in for a mountain bike to arrive at a figure for frame size. Check this figure against manufacturers' online catalogues, then visit a bike shop to ensure correct fit.

Here are other factors to take into account:

Riding style: road riders sit in the same position for long periods of time, mountain bike riders don't, so they may prefer a smaller, more manoeuvrable frame than is usually recommended for casual riders.

Crank length: most bikes come with 170mm cranks as standard. Shorter riders may benefit from shorter cranks and taller riders from longer ones. This isn't written in stone, however, as Lance Armstrong, seven times winner of the Tour de France, favours short cranks and a high cadence (rate of pedal revolutions per minute).

Saddle height: sit on the bike and align the pedals with the seat tube, then put your heel on the lower pedal. Adjust the seatpost height until your leg is straight but not locked out at the knee. Once this adjustment is made, the knee should remain slightly bent at the lowest point of each turn of the pedals when the ball of the foot is on the pedal.

Note that a mark on the seatpost indicates how far it can be raised safely. If you exceed that point when adjusting saddle height, you are probably on the wrong size bike.

Saddle Position

Sliding the saddle forward or backward fine-tunes pedalling efficiency. Get someone to help you with this adjustment as you can't do it on your own.

The classic method is to sit on the bike and rotate the pedals until they are parallel to the ground with the right pedal forward. With the ball of your foot on this pedal, the small bump below the knee, called the tibial tuberosity, should be directly above the pedal axle. Ask your helper to use a plumb line to see whether your knee is in the right position. If it isn't, loosen the bolt that secures the saddle to the seatpost and adjust the

saddle forward or backward, then check the knee position again. Once you are satisfied, retighten the saddle, making sure it is horizontal.

Reach: the distance between saddle and handlebars, this is critical for comfort and depends on top tube and stem length. Modern stems, which clamp around the top of the bike fork's steering column and the handlebars, vary in length and angle, allowing scope for fine-tuning position.

Newcomers to cycling should start off with their handlebars set just below the height of the saddle so, with a straight back and elbows slightly bent, the muscles of the abdomen rather than the arms are supporting your upper body weight. If the back feels overstretched, the first thing to do is fit a shorter stem, which a good bike shop will do when you are buying the bike.

Aerodynamics shouldn't be a big concern at this point. As you grow more used to the bike, the stem can be lowered by removing one of the spacers below it. Doing this, though, means the steerer column will need to be cut down, a job best left to a bike shop.

Lever position: on a mountain bike, the brake and gear levers should be set up so that your arms and wrists are in a straight line. On a road bike, the hands should be able to rest comfortably on

When choosing a new bike, it is important to ensure that the bike fits you rather than you trying to fit the bike.

top of the brake levers.
Feet: if you are using clipless pedals, it is important that the shoe cleats are adjusted to a position that feels natural, reflecting the way you walk, when the ball of the foot is over the pedal axle. Any other position risks knee damage.

Finally, aches and pains in the back, neck and shoulders and numbness in the hands and feet are signs that something is wrong and adjustments need to be made to your riding position. For persistent problems, seek expert advice.

Correct Fit for BMX

BMX bike sizing is based on top tube length not saddle height, and the ideal position is one where you can hold the handlebars without feeling overstretched or cramped. Any drastic change in the angle of the handlebars to improve rider position is not advisable as it will affect control.

Test rides are important as bike manufacturers' top tube measurements differ. More helpfully, bikes are divided into categories based on rider height with stem length, handlebar width and rise, tyre width and crankarm length increasing proportionately as riders get taller.

Rider height	Frame size	Top tube length
4ft and under	Micro-Mini	15in to 15.5in
4ft to 4ft 6in	Mini	15.5in to 16.5in
4ft 4in to 4ft 10in	Junior	16in to 17.5in
4ft 8in to 5ft 4in	Expert	17in to 18.5in
5ft 2in to 5ft 8in	Expert XL	18in to 19in
5ft 6in to 5ft 10in	Pro	18.5in to 19.5in
5ft 10in to 6ft 1in	Pro XL	19in to 21in
6ft plus	Pro XXL	20.5in plus, usually custom-made

Clothing and accessories

Practical clothing, designed for performance, won't automatically make you a better rider but it will make you a less sweaty, better-protected and more comfortable one – and that can only improve your enjoyment of cycling.

Helmet

An essential purchase, modern helmets are light, well-ventilated and comfortable. Apart from specialist full-face and aerodynamic helmets, there are two main types: road and mountain bike, the latter offering greater protection at the back of the head. A helmet must fit and be worn correctly in order to work – the best have a rear retention system – and are designed to withstand a single impact, so always replace a damaged helmet after an accident.

Shorts

Trousers with seams chafe and can cause rashes and boils in the groin, so invest in seamless Lycra shorts. They have a synthetic chamois insert for comfort, are cut high to cover the lower back and are worn without underwear.

Jersey

Cut long to cover the lower back and with pockets at the rear, jerseys are made of breathable fabrics that wick sweat away from the body.

Shoes

Cycling shoes have a stiff sole to protect the foot and most have Velcro straps rather than laces to avoid tangles. Mountain bike and road shoes are available for clipless pedal systems, which feature a cleat on the sole of the shoe that locks onto the pedal, improving pedalling efficiency. The lock disengages with a flick of the ankle. Off-road shoes are a good first choice as, unlike road shoes, they are designed for both walking and riding. Even with toeclips, a stiff-soled shoe is a must.

Gloves and Glasses

Leather-palmed track mitts cushion your hands from handlebar vibrations and protect the palms in a fall. Sunglasses will protect your eyes from grit, bugs and anything else that might fly at you during a ride. Pairs with interchangeable lenses can be worn year-round.

Winter Gear

To keep warm and dry in winter, wear several thin layers of clothes that trap warm air between them, insulating the body. The base layer should be a long-sleeved vest of a material that wicks moisture away from the skin. A long-sleeved cycling jersey or short-sleeved jersey with arm-warmers comes next, topped by a wind- and waterproof jacket, again made of breathable material. Opt for either shorts and leg-warmers or tights that feature windproof panels for the legs for extra protection.

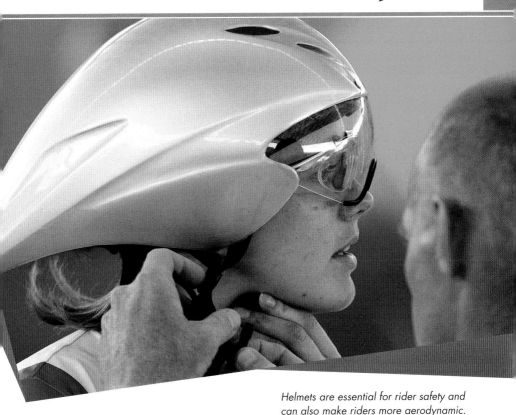

Helmets are essential for rider safety and can also make riders more aerodynamic.

Wear a beanie cap, headband or balaclava under your helmet, full-finger gloves thin enough that you can easily work brakes and gears on your hands and a pair of Neoprene overshoes that fit over your cycling shoes to keep your feet dry.

BMX Kit

BMX racing requires full-face helmets which don't come cheap but offer great protection. Knee and elbow pads are designed to protect the joints while allowing them to move freely, and to protect your hands choose between mitts and full-finger gloves. All are padded at the palm, with the best ones including knuckle padding and protective Kevlar reinforcement.

Jerseys are loose-fitting and long-sleeved and made of a tear-resistant fabric, although Lycra is banned at top races. For trousers, choose between long trousers with a loose fit everywhere except the ankles or loose-fitting shorts accompanied by knee and shin pads. No special shoes are required, although strong soles are an advantage.

Basic maintenance

Tour de France legend Eddy Merckx used to wake up in the night to make minor adjustments to his bike. He knew victory depended on a well-maintained machine. Learning how to repair your bike will save money and headaches, and the satisfaction of a job well done is a welcome bonus, too.

Attend a Bike Maintenance Course

The best advice for anyone who knows nothing about cycle maintenance is to go on a course and learn about it. Local cycling campaign groups, adult and community colleges and many bike shops run practical, hands-on courses for beginners. Alternatively, look online where a number of websites have illustrated guides to all aspects of bike repair.

A Quick Bike Check

Prevention is better than cure. Get into the habit of giving your bike a quick inspection after every ride to identify potential problems so they can be sorted out early.

Tyres: press each tyre with your thumb and, if there is any give, pump them up. Inspect the tread and sidewall for signs of wear or damage. Remove any fragments of glass or thorns embedded in the tread.

Wheels: grab the rim and push it from side to side to check for hub problems. Then spin the wheel fairly slowly and watch the rim as it passes the brake blocks. If there is any wobble, the wheel may need to be trued.

Brakes: squeeze the levers to check they work and, as you do this, look at the brake blocks front and rear. Properly aligned, the whole face of each block should hit the rim.

Cables: make sure the cable ends aren't frayed and check the cables are properly seated in the levers, brakes and derailleurs.

Essential toolkit

Carrying tools on every ride is a necessity, particularly off-road. A mechanical problem can quickly turn into something much more serious when you are a long way from civilisation. The basic minimum is a puncture repair kit, two or three tyre levers, a spare inner tube because some punctures are just too big to patch, a good pump that fits the valves on the bike, bike spanners, allen keys, chain link extractor and spoke key.

Also consider investing in a multitool. Like a cycling version of the Swiss army knife, it contains many essential repair tools in one convenient package.

Bottom bracket and chainset: grab the crankarms and rock them from side to side. Any movement is a sign of potential trouble.

Headset: lift the front wheel off the ground and rotate the bars from side to side. The movement should be smooth without any tightness or excessive play.

Nuts and bolts: everything should be tight. A quick test is to lift the bike a couple of inches off the ground then drop it. If anything rattles, locate and tighten it. Give a closer inspection to the wheelnuts or quick releases securing the wheels to the frame.

Regular Maintenance

Dirt is the enemy of moving parts. Mountain bikers need to clean and lubricate their bikes after every off-road ride; others can get by with doing this once a month, though many cyclists make it a weekly routine. In either case, pay particular attention to the drivetrain. Chains stretch and need regular replacement. Left undetected, a worn chain will damage the teeth of the chainring and rear sprockets, which are expensive to replace.

It is a good habit to give your bike a thorough inspection after every ride.

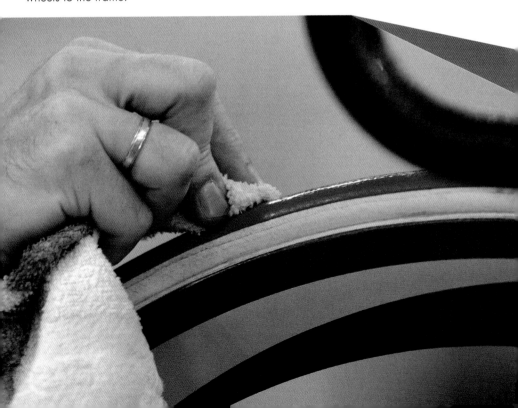

Basic riding

Top riders are at one with their bikes, cycling with confidence, efficiency and economy of effort. So think about where your technique needs improvement, then work on those areas one by one to develop a smooth riding style.

Pedalling

The world is divided into spinners and mashers. Spinners use the body's supply of energy efficiently and conserve its reserves of power for the times when they are needed. Mashers stomp down hard on the pedals and run out of energy quickly. It pays to learn how to spin.

Cadence

Cadence is the number of times a cyclist turns the cranks per minute. Casual cyclists don't give any thought to this figure, but serious cyclists do, because pedalling slowly uses more energy than pedalling fast.

Turning the pedals involves applying force to them. Lower revolutions per minute (rpm) requires more force than higher revolutions per minute. This puts greater demands on the legs' muscles, tendons and joints and speeds the build-up of lactic acid in muscles, which fatigues the legs and makes them hurt.

Faster pedalling with less pressure – spinning – works the cardiovascular system. One of its functions is to move lactic acid from the muscles, so the legs get less tired and can work for longer. Maintaining a higher cadence has another advantage, too – it makes it easier to accelerate.

Measuring Cadence

Every rider has a day-to-day cadence they employ without thinking. Several cycle computers on the market feature a cadence sensor that makes this easy to measure. Otherwise, find a flat, traffic-free stretch of road and, cycling at your usual speed, use a watch as a timer to count how many revolutions one leg pedals in 30 seconds. Multiply that number by two for your average cadence.

Improving Cadence

One easy way to do this is to time how long it takes to ride a route you know well at your usual cadence. The next time you ride it, tackle a short section in a lower gear with a view to covering the

Better pedalling

The downstroke is the most obviously active part of each turn of the pedals. Letting the legs do nothing on the upstroke, though, isn't efficient, so experienced cyclists pull up on the upstroke as well as pushing down on the downstroke.

The way to do this is to lift the heel at the bottom of the downstroke and, as former Tour de France winner Greg Lemond succinctly put it, pretend to scrape mud off the sole of your shoe during the upstroke.

Flexing the ankle in this way feels unnatural at first and it takes time for the body to adapt to the technique. Once you have perfected it, though, you will notice how efficient it is in delivering power to the drivetrain.

Learning to pedal efficiently will help you conserve your energy for when it is needed.

full distance in the same time. With each ride, gradually lengthen the low-gear section until you complete the whole journey in the lower gear. Your body will have grown used to the quicker pedalling tempo and you can then slowly extend how far you can ride at this cadence.

Alternatively, you can gradually build up your spinning on a ride like this by increasing cadence by 5 rpm each week or fortnight. It's important, though, never to bounce about in the saddle as you pedal – a sure sign you are spinning too fast, which will quickly tire you out.

The cadence of BMX riders and sprinters can benefit from doing intervals. Once warmed up on a ride, pedal as fast as possible for a minute, then relax and ride easily for three or four minutes, then sprint again. A couple of bursts is enough the first time. As your body gets used to it, gradually add more bursts up to a maximum of six.

	Typical cadences
Casual cycling:	60–80 rpm
Road racing and time trialling:	80–120rpm
Mountain bike racing:	80–90rpm
BMX, Track and Road sprinting:	up to 170 rpm

Gearing

Gears exist to deliver power to the rear wheel and to help you maintain a steady speed through changes in terrain and wind direction. No matter what bike you ride, your choice of gear is important. Picking the right one makes cycling much easier and more enjoyable.

Gears

Imagine you have gone on a ride and stopped midway at a café. Refuelled, you start riding again and, as luck would have it, you have a tailwind, so soon you are sailing along at a comfortable cadence in high gear.

Two miles later, you realise you left your wallet at the café. When you turn back, the wind is against you. To stay in the same gear and maintain the same cadence is hard work. Shift into a gear low enough to maintain cadence and you will recover your wallet without feeling exhausted.

The trade-off is that on the return leg you won't travel as far per pedal revolution as on the outward leg.

A gear is determined by the number of teeth on the chainset and on the rear cog or sprocket. Bikes are equipped with gears to suit the riding they are expected to do. Mountain bikes have a wide range of low gears for tackling rough terrain and steep climbs. Road and time trial bikes have a narrow range of high gears to accommodate minor variations in gradient and wind while maintaining speed.

Even on single-gear BMX and track bikes, cogs and chainrings can be replaced to suit a rider's needs. A racing BMX has a higher gear than a freestyle bike, while a Keirin rider may favour a lower gear than a sprinter on the track.

Measuring gears

It is worth knowing how to measure gears because in some branches of the sport there are restrictions on gear size. There are different ways to do this:

- **Gear ratio:** the number of teeth on the front chainring divided by the number of teeth on the rear cog.
- **Gear inches:** the number of teeth on the front chainring divided by the number of teeth on the rear cog multiplied by the diameter of the rear wheel. This figure represents the the front wheel diameter of a penny-farthing with equivalent gearing and is useful for comparison purposes.
- **Metres of development:** the number of teeth on the front chainring divided by the number of teeth on the rear cog multiplied by the circumference of the rear wheel in millimetres. This figure represents how far a bike travels in one revolution of the cranks.
- Since tyre size affects the diameter and circumference of the wheel, the maths can get complicated. Luckily, other people have already done the work for you. For information visit the Cyclists' Touring Club website, ctc.org.uk

Bad Gear Shifts

Chains should travel in straight lines. Running a chain from the large chainring at the front to the large cog at the back, or the small front chainring to the small rear cogs, bends it sideways. Avoid doing this as it wears the chain and the chainring and sprocket teeth and can make the chain rub against the front derailleur cage.

Derailleurs are designed to work when you are pedalling. If you shift them when you aren't, when you resume pedalling they will change gear accompanied by grating noises and possibly a thrown chain.

Good Gear Shifts

Slightly reduce the pressure on the pedals when you change gears. When the chain is under less tension, it shifts more smoothly.

Gear levers are at your fingertips to make it easy to use them. Don't forget to change gear as often as required to maintain a steady cadence. When you find yourself putting more pressure on the pedals, shift into a lower gear. When your legs can't keep up with the pedals, shift into a higher gear.

Learn to anticipate, so you can be in the right gear at the right time. The most practical gear shift to anticipate is an everyday one. As you approach a road junction or traffic lights, change into a lower gear before you stop. Starting will be much easier and you can quickly build up speed before changing into a higher gear.

Choosing the right gear at the right time can make the difference between victory and defeat.

Riding in a group

Riding with other people not only adds to your enjoyment of cycling, but also teaches you valuable lessons about bike handling and the etiquette of the bunch. Even when gold medals are at stake, cyclists follow certain rules of behaviour for reasons of safety and survival.

Choose carefully: cycling clubs, campaign groups and bike shops all organise rides, so you should find plenty in your area. Contact the organiser to find out about the ride's route, mileage and food stops, if any. Ask about the group's composition in terms of age and experience and whether newcomers are welcome. Pick easy rides at first to gain experience and improve fitness.

Be punctual: arrive late for the start and you may meet several grumpy people or find the ride left without you.

Carry the kit: arrive with a basic toolkit for emergency repairs, appropriate clothing, a mobile phone and some money. Should you lose contact with the group, you need to be self-sufficient.

Obey the law: the rules of the road, such as obeying traffic signals, apply to group training rides.

Be predictable: avoid any sudden movements, such as getting out of the saddle, or changes in direction that might affect riders beside and behind you. They have to trust you. Avoid looking over your shoulder, too, as this makes your bike change direction.

Don't brake suddenly: have your fingers on the brake levers at all times. Brake gently and smoothly to give following riders time to brake too.

Develop double vision: continually watch both the wheel immediately ahead of you and the front of the group to monitor its movements. You don't want to be out of position when the group swings out to avoid a pothole or lines up to take a corner.

Don't overlap: your front wheel overlapping the wheel ahead of you invites trouble. If it moves off its line and the wheels touch, you may fall – and bring down riders behind you. It's safest to position your front wheel a few inches behind and to one side of the wheel in front of you.

Prepare for contact: shoulders often rub in tight groups. It's important not to flinch when it happens. If the idea unnerves you, ride somewhere quiet with a friend and practise riding shoulder-to-shoulder.

This is also a useful drill for BMX racers and mountain bikers, who often touch at the start of races.

Pass the message: the riders at front and back use calls and hand signals to warn the group about potential hazards. It's everyone's responsibility to pass on information as well as announce when they are about to do something that will affect other riders.

For safety's sake, vigilance and good communication are essential when riding in a group.

Training

The cycling bug has bitten and you want to ride longer and faster than you do now. That involves riding yourself into the ground, right? Wrong. Adopt a sensible approach to training and you will enjoy cycling more and still succeed in your ambitions.

What do you want to achieve?

One of cycling's big attractions is you can mix it up, because the path to fitness is broadly similar for all branches of the sport. Olympic champion Sir Chris Hoy, for example, started his racing career in BMX before switching to Track.

Decide on Your Goals

Perhaps, for now, you dream of excelling in just one cycling discipline – you will need a plan to realise that dream. A successful sports career is built in stages based around short-, medium- and long-term goals with concrete targets that you can work towards and hit.

Start by being honest about how often you ride and how much time you can devote to cycling. Even if you cycle every day as a commuter, go out for slightly longer weekend rides for a few weeks and see how they fit into your schedule. Then consider where you want to be in the sport in four or five years – your long-term goal – and how any life changes might affect this.

Next, look at what you want to achieve in the next year, your mid-term goals. Set targets specific to you and keep them modest at first – finishing in the top half of the field in your first mountain bike race, for example. If you have never raced before, it's also a good idea to target a specific competitive event for your debut, so you can build up to it. Plan this well in advance, so you have plenty of time to prepare.

Find a Coach

Once you have a clear idea of what you want to achieve, seek out a qualified coach who can help you to draw up a detailed plan split into four- to eight-week training periods that will equip you with

Training's basic principle

Cycle training is based on the principle of progressive overload. By starting slowly and gradually increasing the amount of exercise you do, the body adapts to each increase in workload and becomes more efficient. You exercise, your body becomes fatigued, you give it time to recover and adjust to that level of exertion. Next time you ask a bit more of your body, it becomes fatigued, you give it time to recover and adapt and so on.

It's important to concentrate on gradual progression rather than overload – think in terms of months rather than weeks. Push too hard too quickly and you will lay yourself open to illness and injuries. On the other hand, if you don't keep ramping up the effort bit by bit you will hit a plateau where your body feels comfortable but your fitness isn't improving.

Identify some short-, medium- and long-term goals that you can work towards and hit.

short-term goals designed to deliver the strength, power, endurance and skills to achieve your mid-term goals.

The reason for setting modest initial targets is simple. Hitting them will bring personal satisfaction, which will keep you motivated to aim a little higher next time. You and your coach can always revise mid-term goals as your fitness and performance improve.

The body in training

The world's most advanced computer doesn't come close to matching the complexity of the human body. Once you start taking cycling seriously, it pays dividends to know a little bit about how training works and how it affects the body.

Aerobic and Anaerobic Exercise

Fitness can be broadly divided into two categories: endurance and power. The two are linked because of the ways the body stores and uses its fuel supplies, so a cyclist's training programme is typically designed to improve both.

Exercise comes in two forms: aerobic, which means with oxygen, is for endurance and stamina building, and anaerobic, without oxygen, is for power. Aerobic exercise is lower in intensity and much longer in duration than anaerobic exercise. How the body reacts and adapts to these two forms varies from individual to individual, according to their genetic make-up and age.

Energy Supplies

Our bodies break down food and store the chemicals it contains for use as fuel in three ways:

Aerobic system: during steady rides, fuels drawn from carbohydrates – mainly glucose and its stored form, glycogen – and fats react with oxygen supplied by the blood to synthesise adenosine triphosphate (ATP), a chemical that releases energy to fire the muscles' slow-twitch fibres. The body has a limited store of ATP but, by synthesising the chemical, it keeps the supply topped up.

Anaerobic lactic system: when high-intensity effort is required a different series of chemical reactions occur that produce both ATP and lactic acid, a waste product that after 10–60 seconds accumulates in the muscles and makes them hurt, a feeling that continues until the effort is reduced and oxygen delivery to the muscles returns to normal.

Anareobic alactic system: at maximum-exercise intensity the body uses phosphocreatine to make

What is VO_2 max?

VO_2 max (also called aerobic capacity) is a cyclist's performance ceiling, the largest amount of oxygen the body can transport and use during maximum exercise effort. Measured in millilitres of oxygen per kilogram per minute, VO_2 is tested on a cycle ergometer that records oxygen intake and use while the effort of cycling is gradually increased to the point of exhaustion. VO_2 max increases with training, though the rate of improvement varies from person to person.

ATP. Muscle stores of this chemical are so small that effort can only be sustained for 6–10 seconds before fatigue kicks in and the body takes longer to return to normal.

Aerobic Exercise Benefits
- Stronger lungs
- Stronger heart
- Burns fat
- Better blood circulation
- Raised red blood cell count
- Better mental health
- Improved aerobic metabolism
- Quicker recovery

Anaerobic Exercise Benefits
- Improves fuel storage
- Burns fat
- Strengthens bones and joints
- Strengthens cardiovascular system
- Raises anaerobic threshold

Understanding the impact certain types of exercise has on your body will help you reach your training goals.

Turning Points in Exercise
The adult body has two key turning points where it switches from one energy system to another. These points are not fixed and with training they can be improved, allowing you to perform at higher intensity for longer periods of time. The lactate threshold of an average person is at about 60 per cent of their VO_2 max, while in an elite athlete it can be at 85–90 per cent of VO_2 max.

Aerobic threshold: the point where the anaerobic pathways start to operate, usually at about 65 per cent of maximum heart rate. Riding just below this point is good for aerobic endurance and above it for short-term muscular endurance.
Lactate threshold: also called anaerobic threshold, this is reached when the muscles produce lactic acid at a faster rate than the body can remove it – usually at about 85–90 per cent of maximum heart rate. Riding above this point cannot be sustained for more than a few seconds before exhaustion sets in.

Training safely

Whether you ride on road or off, safety is of paramount importance when cycling. No rider wants an activity that gives them so much pleasure to end in illness or injury, so every time you throw your leg over the bike and prepare to go for a ride be alive to the potential dangers.

Stay Alert

Find a traffic-free location such as a playground for practising specific skills such as track stands and bunny-hops. On every ride, alone or with others, stay aware of what's going on around you. Traffic, pedestrians, other cyclists, animals, potholes, drain covers, roadworks and changes in road and trail surfaces are just some of the potential hazards. By staying alert, you give yourself time to avoid problems. Watch out for the weather, too. Wet and windy conditions can turn even the most familiar route into a dicey prospect.

Easy Does It

Smart training is structured, with the frequency of sessions and their duration rationed out so a rider not only gains fitness but also remains enthusiastic about the sport. Do too much and you risk losing motivation and suffer from overtraining.

The first sign of overtraining is a loss of form, an inability to perform as well as expected. Other symptoms include a higher heart rate when exercising at low intensity; a greater feeling of fatigue between training sessions; sore, tender muscles; problems with sleeping and relaxing; loss of weight and appetite; and all-round grumpiness and irritability. Overtraining also weakens the body's

Basic ride safety checklist

Do these important checks to avoid self-inflicted wounds:

- Bike – inspect your bike regularly to ensure it is in perfect working order. The ears are a great diagnostic tool, so when you ride listen out for any noises coming from the bike that indicate parts are rubbing or loose. Do any repairs as soon as possible.
- Clothing – avoid wearing loose clothing on the bike and tuck shoelaces into shoes, because it is easy for loose fabric to get snagged in a bike's moving parts.
- Helmet – make sure it is the right size for your head and is fitted properly with the straps joining just under the ear to form a neat V and the two sets of straps fastened under the chin. A helmet should move around very little on the head when correctly adjusted.

immune system, making you more
susceptible to illness.

   When form dips, it is tempting to think
you aren't doing enough training and
try to do more. This will only worsen the
situation – instead, back off and look
carefully at what you have been doing
to get into this state. It may be you have
been taking too much exercise and
allowing too little recovery time or have
been training while suffering from a cold,

*Top level athletes and their coaches constantly
monitor performance for signs of overtraining.*

flu or bronchitis. Rest may resolve the
problem, allowing the body's defences
to do their work. Otherwise, seek advice
from your coach, who may recommend
consulting a doctor or pharmacist for
specific treatment.

Training plans and diaries

Having a plan for your riding is essential to improve performance, to keep you motivated and to avoid the risk of overtraining. It's also very important to keep a record of the exercise you do and how you were feeling when you did it, so you can keep on track with your plan and monitor progress.

Training Plans

Training plans are like made-to-measure suits – what fits one person won't fit someone else. So much depends on the individual genetic make-up, initial level of fitness and sporting ambitions that it is impossible to deliver a one-size-fits-all routine. The one constant for training, however, is fitness, which is a combination of six elements.

Six Components of Fitness

- **Aerobic endurance:** steady, low-intensity riding builds aerobic endurance, allowing you to do more while using less energy, a particularly important requirement for Road and Mountain Bike racing and the Individual and Team pursuit on the track.
- **Short-term muscular endurance:** short, high-intensity activities such as BMX racing require the ability to put out a lot of power for a limited period of time.
- **Strength:** climbing hills, riding off-road, even braking on downhills all require strength.
- **Muscle power:** strength is one part of this; how quickly muscles contract is the other. Together they produce great power over a very short period of time, which is required in any form of massed-start racing as well as in sprints.

- **Speed:** this depends on the ability to pedal at high cadence and change cadence quickly, key components in all forms of cycling.
- **Flexibility:** if the joints aren't flexible or the muscles too constricted, it has an impact on bike handling skills and comfort, both of which affect performance.

The balance between the six varies from individual to individual and on the requirements of the branch of the sport. A coach will aim to prescribe a training plan that addresses any problems you have that affect performance. This doesn't just include fitness. Skills, technique, mental preparation and basics such as riding position will all come under scrutiny.

Training Diary

A plan gives structure to your cycling, a diary keeps track of it. It's a motivational and an analytical tool, a record of what you have achieved and how you felt while doing it. The first pieces of information to put into your diary are your goals. Other details to add on a daily basis include:

- **Heart rate:** take your pulse first thing in the morning as it is a good indicator of your general physical wellbeing. A heart rate more than 8–10 beats above or below your average figure is a sign you may be coming down with an illness or be tired and need a rest day. If you use a heart rate monitor while training, add details of those figures too.

- **General mood:** noting how you feel physically and mentally gives an indication of your recovery time after training and how outside factors such as work can affect performance. Jot down how you felt during each ride, too, which helps to show how well you are adapting to exercise.
- **Training:** recording details of a ride's duration, distance, intensity, weather, terrain, average speed, whether you were riding solo or in a group and the route will help to keep you motivated and encourage variety.
- **Sleep:** keep track of how long and how well you sleep each night to aid the recovery process.
- **Weight:** stepping on to the scales once or twice a week monitors your diet, while a sharp drop in weight may be a sign of dehydration.
- **Diet:** keeping track of your diet lets you see which foods work best for you. Note what you eat and drink too before, during and after a ride.

Training Plan Elements

At first glance, just about the only things the two sample plans on page 64 have in common are rest days. Recovery time is crucial for performance, allowing the body to adapt to the exercise requirements placed on it and preparing it to face future demands. Look at the plans more closely, though, and you will see that both specify how often, how hard and how long both riders should be training. This is the FIT Principle – Frequency, Intensity and Time – that coaches use to improve fitness levels.

Regular Exercise

The performance benefits for newcomers to the sport start to kick in when cycling three days a week, with more experienced competitive riders usually graduating to training five days a week. Over time, both the intensity and duration of rides, and specific exercises within them, increase too.

Patience is a Virtue

Patience isn't a word that features in many training manuals, though it ought to. Accept that getting fit is achieved through lots of small steps taken over months and concentrate on enjoying the riding that you do along the way.

Sample Training Plans

While any cyclist can enjoy participating in different branches of the sport, the training demands of specific cycling disciplines vary widely – it's safe to assume that the training regimes for Sir Chris Hoy's Olympic Games Track Sprint final and a Tour de France winner are very different.

Time Triallist: Pre-season

Monday:	Rest day.
Tuesday:	1 hour 15 minutes ride. 15 minutes warm-up, then 2 sets of 3x3 minutes riding as hard as possible, 5 minutes of recovery between efforts, and 10 minutes recovery between sets, followed by 10 minutes of easy pedalling to cool down.
Wednesday:	Rest day.
Thursday:	1 hour ride. 15 minutes warm-up, then time trial pace, followed by 10 minutes cooling down.
Friday:	Rest day.
Saturday:	1 hour ride, 15 minutes warm up, then 6 sets of 3 minutes of high cadence spinning, 3 minutes recovery between sets, rest of ride at cooling down pace.
Sunday:	3.5 hours ride. Steady, low-intensity pace.

BMX: Mid-season

Monday:	Rest day.
Tuesday:	1 hour. Sprint training. 10 minutes warm-up, then 2 sets of 20 seconds x 6 rolling-start sprints, with 4 minutes of recovery between efforts and 8 minutes of recovery between sets, followed by 10 minutes cooling down.
Wednesday:	45 minutes. Gym. Two circuits of strength-building exercises such as squats, leg curls, step-ups and pull-ups, with recovery time between each exercise and a 5-minute break between circuits.
Thursday:	1 hour. Sprint training. 10 minutes warm-up, then 2 sets of 30 seconds x 4 standing-start sprints, going flat out for first 10 seconds then at 80% intensity for 20 seconds, with 4 minutes of recovery between efforts and 10 minutes of recovery between sets, followed by 10 minutes cooling down.
Friday:	1 hour. Track session, focusing on skill development such as cornering, plus 2 circuits of the track at race pace with 8 minutes recovery between them.
Saturday:	Rest day.
Sunday:	Racing

To be a winner requires careful
planning and steady progress.

Measuring performance

Serious competitive riders closely monitor their progress in training. The tools to do this may range from the subjective to the scientific, but all provide important information. By studying your performance, you can adjust your training regime so that you ride to the best of your ability.

Breathing and Talk Test

To develop aerobic and anaerobic fitness, you have to know where the dividing line lies between the two and how far above or below the line you are as you ride. How you feel and how easy or hard it is to breathe gives some indication of this. For many cyclists, this is all the information they require.

The talk test is the simplest measure of effort. When out on a ride with a friend, if you can talk normally without pausing for breath, you aren't riding hard enough.

When you can hold a conversation but need to pause for breath every couple of sentences, you are exercising aerobically. If all you can manage are single-word

Borg Scale of Perceived Exertion Table

Zones	Feeling	6–20 Borg scale	1–10 simplified scale
Recovery	Slow pace, easy spin	6	1
Recovery	Slow pace, easy spin	7	1
Cruise	Relaxed pace	8	2
Cruise	Relaxed pace	9	3
Aerobic	Light pace	10	3
Aerobic	Fairly light, still able to hold a conversation	11	3
Aerobic	Moderate pace, deeper breaths	12–13	3+
Sub Threshold	Moderately hard, broken conversation	14	4–5
Sub Threshold	Moderately hard	14–15	6
Sub Threshold	Hard	15–16	6
Threshold	Deep breathing	16	6–7
Threshold	Very hard	17	7+
VO_2	Laboured breathing, painful muscles	18	8
VO_2+	Extremely hard	19	9
Max	Exhaustion	20	10

responses and broken conversation, you are exercising anaerobically.

Borg Scale of Perceived Exertion

A step up from the talk test, although still subjective, is the Borg Scale of Perceived Exertion, which measures effort on a scale from six to 20, though many people use a simplified version that runs from one to 10.

The tools for measuring performance range from the subjective to the scientific, but all provide important information.

For a more sophisticated way to measure performance, you can invest in either a heart rate monitor or a power meter.

Power Meter

What it does: shows how much power you produce, expressed in Watts, which is then used to calculate your power output as Watts per kilo of body weight.

How it works: strain gauges measure power supplied to the rear wheel and relays details of your current, maximum and average power output, heart rate and speed to a handlebar-mounted monitor. Rival systems mount the gauges in different positions: the cranks, rear hub or chain. Instead of using strain gauges, one system measures opposing forces such as wind resistance, gravity and velocity to calculate power.

Advantages: properly calibrated, power meters provide more accurate measurements than heart rate monitors for setting training targets. They help to develop constant power, a boon for time triallists. Any sudden decline in power output is a clear indication of fatigue, overtraining or illness. Data can also be used to test the impact on performance of different equipment and rider positions.

Disadvantages: expense. Power meters cost more than most entry-level bikes.

Heart Rate Monitor

What it does: records the number of heartbeats per minute during exercise.

How it works: a chest strap reads your heart rate and sends this information to a monitor worn on the wrist or mounted on the handlebars. In most models, this doubles as a cycle computer with details of current and average speed and distance travelled.

Advantages: price. The cheapest models are a small fraction of the cost of a power meter. They allow you to set the target zones where you want your heart rate to be during training sessions, show how long you are in that zone and indicate, either visually or by beeping, if your heart rate moves out of it.

Disadvantages: less accurate than power meters, as heart rate does not always follow effort, especially early in a training session. Also, heart rate can vary depending on altitude, weather, health and state of mind, making it harder to compare similar training rides from day to day.

Buying a Heart Rate Monitor

The affordability of a heart rate monitor makes it the tool of choice for most amateur cyclists. Whatever you buy, look out for a couple of things:

Power meters and heart rate monitors can provide a precise means of measuring performance.

Computer compatibility: you need to be able to download data from the monitor to your computer. Ask a coach, experienced rider or sales assistant about the software available for the heart rate monitor you intend to buy.

Information overload: don't let the monitor's many functions distract you from the ride. If you do, you may come a cropper.

Heart rates differ: your best friend will have a different heart rate to you, so don't try to train at the same rate. Concentrate on measuring performance in terms of where you were, where you are now and where you want to be.

Training in zones

Success as a competitive cyclist calls for a patient, methodical approach to building aerobic and anaerobic fitness. The scientific way to do this is to train in zones of effort intensity, ensuring that the time you spend on your bike is quality time that will produce results rather than wasted effort.

Zones of Effort

Coaches divide exercise into zones of effort intensity. These are expressed as bands of percentages either below maximum heart rate – the fastest rate in beats per minute that your heart can beat – or above your maximum heart rate but below your lactate threshold – the point that divides aerobic from anaerobic exercise.

Both maximum heart rate and lactate threshold vary from person to person. Yet, while some coaches still devise training plans based on maximum heart rate, sports scientists now prefer to use lactate threshold as the key figure for calculating zones of effort, partly because raising your lactate threshold allows you to ride at higher efforts for longer periods of time and to recover more quickly. For the Lactate Threshold Training Zones see page 72.

Finding Your Lactate Threshold (LT)

First it should be emphasised that training based on lactate threshold isn't suitable for children, because they don't produce lactic acid in the same way as adults and are less aware of the signs of impending exhaustion.

If you are an adult, the way to find your lactate threshold is to ride a time trial while wearing a heart rate monitor.

Scout out a flat or slightly uphill stretch of road that's as traffic-free as possible. On a day when you are rested, warm up for 15 minutes at aerobic pace, then ride for 30 minutes as hard and fast as possible. Use the heart rate monitor to record the last 20 minutes of the ride. The average heart rate recorded for this period is the heart rate at lactate threshold. For greater accuracy, repeat the exercise in similar weather conditions after a few days' recovery and take an average of the two figures.

If you don't have a heart rate monitor, you can estimate where your lactate threshold is using the Borg Scale of Perceived Exertion (see page 66). It's the point where breathing is hard but before the legs feel the painful burning sensation caused by lactic acid.

Length of Time in LT Zones

Thinking of the LT zones (see page 73) as an equilateral triangle with zones 1 and 2 at the bottom and zone 5 at the top gives an indication of the relative amount of time spent in each zone. At the bottom, rides are measured in hours and minutes; at the top, high-intensity sprints and intervals are measured in seconds. How to divide time working in different zones depends on the individual and their chosen discipline, which is why advice from a qualified coach is so important.

Seasonal Training

The racing season for most cycling disciplines is in summer, so in winter devote time to building an aerobic endurance base with zone 2 and some zone 3 riding. Once that is in place, in spring and summer continue with zone 2 and 3 rides but also start to spend more time further up the pyramid with shorter, high-intensity rides and interval workouts to raise the lactate threshold and add speed and power, with correspondingly longer recovery times between each ride. The aim is to be in great shape when the racing season begins.

Lactate Threshold Training Zones

Taking your heart rate reading from the time trial test (see pages 70–71) as 100% of lactate threshold (LT), the heart rate for other levels of effort can be calculated as percentages of this figure. Heart rate monitors can be set to beep if your heart rate strays outside the zone where you are meant to be riding, which is one reason why they are useful training tools.

Zone 1: 65–81% of LT – Recovery

Rides at this gentle level don't qualify as aerobic exercise, but perform the valuable function of removing waste products from the muscles and resupplying them with oxygen and fuel. For that reason, competitive cyclists typically schedule a ride of about an hour's duration at this level the day after a race or a high-intensity training session.

Zone 2: 82–88% of LT – Aerobic Endurance

All competitive cyclists spend a lot of time in this zone to build a sound foundation of aerobic endurance. It's the longest ride of the week. Riding at this level increases the number and density of blood vessels in the muscles, stimulates neural responses and trains the body to perform for long stretches of time by strengthening the heart. It's the zone for burning fat, too.

Zone 3: 89–94% of LT – Intensive Aerobic Endurance

While this zone provides similar benefits to zone 2 and improves the cardiorespiratory system, it is also where lactic acid starts to build up in the muscles, so recovery time is required after training in it and all the zones above this level.

Zone 4: 94–99% of LT – Sub Threshold

Lactic acid also builds up in the muscles in this zone, which is characterised by fast-tempo riding and intervals, but by training correctly in it for short periods the body learns to cope with waste products and how to remove them more efficiently. This raises the lactate threshold and brings performance benefits with it.

Methodical training will ensure that you are in prime condition come race day.

Zone 5a: 100–102% of LT
– Above Threshold

This is a zone of fast-tempo riding and interval training similar to zone 4 and produces many of the same benefits. Typically, a rider will train in zone 4 pre-season and early season, then start working more in zone 5 when racing begins.

Zone 5b: 103–105% of LT
– Aerobic Capacity

Riders don't spend much time in this zone of high-intensity intervals and need longer to recover after each session. The benefit it delivers, though, is sustained power, at first for short periods, but gradually, as the body grows used to the effort involved, over longer ones.

Zone 5c: 106% plus of LT
– Anaerobic Capacity

Zone 5c is the power zone, where riders hone the ability to sprint and attack. Because of the intense effort involved, time spent in this zone is measured in seconds and more recovery time is required after each effort.

Diet and hydration

What racing cyclists eat and drink before, during and after a race is every bit as important as the bikes they ride. Food and drink are the fuels that keeps the pedals turning and every cyclist's worst nightmare is running out of energy just when it is needed most.

Diet and Hydration

Cyclists tuck into their food with relish, because anyone who trains regularly finds their dietary needs change and their appetite increases. Quite simply, people who take exercise burn more calories than couch potatoes and those calories need replacing – not just at the end of training or racing but, short sprint events aside, during it too.

Food as Fuel

The food you eat has four main functions:
- It replenishes the fuel stored in the muscles and liver.
- It replaces fluid and electrolytes lost in sweat.
- It bolsters the immune system, making it better equipped to handle the stress of physical exercise.
- It supplies the nutrients necessary for building muscle protein.

What's important is that the body is refuelled with the right ingredients to fulfil these functions. These break down into six main groups:

Carbohydrates

Why they matter: carbohydrates are a major source of glucose, the primary fuel for sustained muscular effort. Carbohydrates come in two forms, complex and simple. Pasta and potatoes, for example, contain the former, which the body takes longer to turn into glucose. Fruit, such as bananas, contain simple carbohydrates that convert quickly into glucose.

Protein

Why it matters: present in every cell of the body, it is in charge of growing and repairing muscles, muscle tissue and blood cells, as well as producing essential enzymes and hormones. Surplus supplies cannot be stored by the body – if you eat too much protein, the body must turn what it doesn't need into energy quickly or else it will convert it into fat.

Fat

Why it matters: it is rich in calories and the primary energy source for low-intensity exercise. It also contains chemicals important for good health. It is present in many foods so we have to limit our intake of it – saturated and trans fats are the unhealthy ones to avoid, while monounsaturated and polyunsaturated fats are good for you, as are the omega-3 fatty acids found in fish.

Vitamins and Minerals

Why they matter: they produce enzymes essential for good health, such as antioxidants that maintain a healthy blood supply. Eating five portions a day of fruit and vegetables should provide all the vitamins and minerals needed. Iron is important for the production of red blood cells, which transport oxygen around the body. Stamina falters and fatigue sets in when iron levels are low. Sodium, potassium and chloride, the electrolyte family of minerals, maintain fluid balance within the body and assist

the transportation of glucose around the body. They are lost in exercise through sweat, one reason why they are key ingredients in energy drinks.

Water
Why it matters: losing water through sweat rapidly affects performance, so it is essential to keep drinking regularly whenever you go for a ride of more than 45 minutes' duration.

Cyclists have long appreciated the need to take on fuel. Here, a rider receives a food bag at the Tokyo 1964 Olympic Games.

What's the Balance?

Eating healthily, particularly salads, steamed vegetables and fresh fruit, should supply all the vitamins and minerals your body needs. The balance between the amount of carbohydrate, protein and fat you consume, however, depends on the kind of cycling you do, your individual DNA and your state of health. Road racers, time triallists and mountain bikers, for example, eat a diet with a high carbohydrate content, because of its energy supply benefits.

To begin with, however, it's enough to be aware of what you eat and to eat healthily – many riders keep a record of their food intake to ensure a well-balanced diet. Once your fitness and performance improve, you may wish to consult a sports nutritionist who will discuss your current eating habits and your training regime and goals with you and then work out an individual diet plan based on the amount of energy needed to meet those goals.

It is important to keep drinking water when cycling for more than 45 minutes.

Race Day Diet Plan

The importance of what a cyclist eats and drink before, during and after a race cannot be understated. The correct food consumed at the right time will ensure they have enough energy to be competitive throughout the race and recover quickly afterwards.

The Week Before

Because carbohydrates play such an important role in endurance events, cyclists fear the drop in blood sugar level that leads to hypoglycaemia – the 'bonk' as cyclists call it – a state of fatigue, weakness and dizziness. To avoid the bonk, carbo-load by increasing the proportion of carbohydrates in your diet in the three days before a race while training less.

The timing of the last big meal before the start is important, too. It's best to allow 15–17 hours for complex carbohydrates to digest and be converted into stored glycogen. Drinking lots of water is also very important, because the body must be fully hydrated. Coffee, tea and alcohol have a dehydrating effect, so they should be avoided.

On Race Day

Eat two to three hours beforehand, concentrating on easily digested, simple carbohydrates such as pasta – leaving the meal any nearer the race start can lead to cramp and upset stomachs. Carbohydrates in this meal won't have time to convert into glycogen but will still provide energy as blood glucose.

During the Race

You need to rehydrate and refuel on any ride lasting more than 45 minutes. Drinking water is essential, preferably both on its own and in an energy drink. The best of these contain carbohydrates, electrolytes and a little bit of protein to help convert carbohydrate to glucose.

Energy drinks vary, so experiment with a few on training rides to settle on one that suits your tastes and needs.

The rule is drink little and often at a time, making sure you take in water before you feel thirsty. How much to drink varies from person to person. It is possible to drink too much, although the risks of drinking too little are much higher. It's not uncommon for Tour de France riders to drink 5 litres of water during the course of a stage – or even more on a hot day.

Food for longer rides needs to be easily digestible and conveniently packaged. Bananas are the classic fruit of choice. Fruit and nut bars are another inexpensive option, and serious athletes opt for energy bars and energy gels, which are designed for quick digestion.

The rule of thumb on any ride is to carry more food and drink than you think you will need. If that's not possible, during a race you will need a helper to hand you up bottles and food supplies, while on a training ride a quick pitstop at a café or shop is often the best solution.

After the Race

Your body needs to recover after all your exertions, so a drink of water to rehydrate is the first priority after you get off the bike. Follow it up quickly with a modest amount of simple carbohydrates and protein – a muesli bar, a bowl of cereal with yogurt and fruit or a ham sandwich, for example – to replenish glucose supplies. Then wait a couple of hours before eating a larger meal, again containing lots of carbohydrates.

Pre-ride stretching

At a big track meeting, competitors spinning away on static bikes and stretching are a common sight. That's because, for even the fittest rider, sudden exercise delivers a shock to the system. The body has to be warmed up first to prepare it for what lies ahead.

Stretching

Stretching before a ride aligns the body, improving flexibility, stimulates blood flow and prepares the muscles, ligaments and tendons for exercise. It's also relaxing, which benefits both mind and body. Before a long ride or a competitive one, it's best to warm up the muscles by going for a gentle 10–15-minute ride, then run through a series of stretches before the main event. Before shorter rides, you may only wish to start with a few gentle stretches.

Technique

It's important to ease muscles into position not bounce them, which can produce tears in muscle tissue. Every move should be slow and deliberate, each position taken to a point of mild tension not pain. Start out by holding each position for the recommended stretch time, breathing

Quadriceps
Stand on the left leg, holding on to a wall or table for support if needed. Slightly bend the right knee and bring the heel toward the buttock without them touching. Reach for the ankle with the right hand. Straighten the knee and feel the stretch in the top of the thigh and hip. Hold for 20–30 seconds, then release and repeat with the left leg.

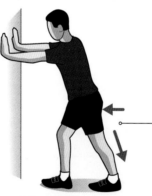

Calf
Stand about an arm's-length from a wall. Place your forearms on the wall and rest your head on your hands. Bend one leg in front of you and extend the other leg behind you with both heels on the ground and toes pointing straight forward. Ease your hips forward until you feel the stretch in the straight leg. Hold for 20 seconds, then switch legs and repeat.

Achilles Tendon
Still leaning against the wall, slightly bend the back knee, keeping the feet flat. Ease the hips forward to feel the stretch lower in your leg. Hold for 10 seconds, then switch legs and repeat.

slowly and rhythmically. Relax, then move back into the stretch for a further 5 seconds, this time moving slightly further into it, again only to a point that is comfortable. If the recommended stretch time feels too long, reduce it. As your body becomes more flexible, you will be able to stretch for longer.

This is a selection of basic stretches to get you started. A qualified coach or fitness instructor can add to the routine, further increasing your flexibility.

Hamstrings
Sit with one leg straight and the other leg bent so the foot touches the thigh of the straight leg. With the back straight and head up, reach toward the toes. Hold for 20 seconds, then repeat with the other leg.

Arms, Shoulders and Upper Back 1
Entwine your fingers above your head, palms upward. Breathing slowly and rhythmically, gradually move your arms backward and upward until you can feel mild tension in the arms and shoulders. Hold for 15–20 seconds.

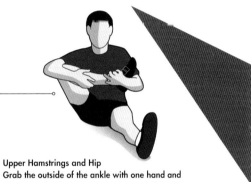

Upper Hamstrings and Hip
Grab the outside of the ankle with one hand and place the other hand and forearm around the bent knee. Slowly pull the whole leg toward the chest, making sure not to stress the knee, until you feel mild tension in the back of the upper leg. Hold for 15–20 seconds, then repeat with the other leg.

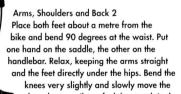

Arms, Shoulders and Back 2
Place both feet about a metre from the bike and bend 90 degrees at the waist. Put one hand on the saddle, the other on the handlebar. Relax, keeping the arms straight and the feet directly under the hips. Bend the knees very slightly and slowly move the chest down until you feel the stretch in the arms, shoulders and back. Hold for 15 seconds, then relax. Coming out of the stretch, avoid back strain by bending the knees further before standing.

Groin
Put the soles of the feet together at a point that feels comfortable. Lightly hold your feet and slowly bend from the hip, not the shoulders, until you feel mild tension in the groin. Hold for 20–30 seconds, then release.

Post-ride stretching

By relaxing and slowly cooling down the muscles and cardiovascular system after exertion, stretching keeps the body supple, reduces soreness and prevents injury. As with pre-ride stretching, the aim is to take muscles to a point of mild tension and not overstretch them.

Hip Flexors
Kneel on the left knee with the right leg in front of you bent at the knee. Put the left hand on the right leg for stability and the right hand on the right hip. Keeping your back straight, lean gently forward to shift body weight on to the front leg until you feel mild tension in the left thigh. Hold the stretch for 20–30 seconds, then repeat with the other leg.

Hip Adductors
Stand with one leg to the side, keeping it straight. Bend the other leg and lean weight on to it. Squat, bending the knee a little further until you feel mild tension on the inside of the thigh of the straight leg. Hold for 15–20 seconds, then release. Repeat with the other leg.

Hamstrings and Lower Back
Lie down with the back of both heels flat to the floor. Slowly pull one knee up to the chest until you feel the stretch in your lower back. Keep the other leg relaxed and comfortable, either extended straight out or with the knee bent and the foot flat on the floor. Bring the raised knee as close to your chest as possible without strain. Hold the stretch for 20–30 seconds, then switch legs and repeat.

Hamstrings
Lie on your back, lift one leg up to form an angle as close as possible to 90 degrees to the ground. The aim is to feel mild tension, not pain, in the back of the thigh. The other leg can either be bent at the knee or straight out, depending on what's more comfortable. As you make the stretch, tilt the pelvis to keep the lower back flat against the floor. Hold the stretch for 15–20 seconds, then repeat with the other leg.

Lower Back
Stand with the knees slightly bent, place the palms of the hands on the lower back just above the hips, fingers pointing downward. Gently push the palms forward to create an extension in the lower back. Hold comfortable pressure for 10–15 seconds. Repeat twice.

Shoulders and Neck
Lift the top of the shoulders toward the ears, as if shrugging, until you feel mild tension in the neck and shoulders. Hold for 3–5 seconds, then relax the shoulders downward into their normal position. Repeat the stretch two or three times.

Sides
With legs apart and arms overhead, grasp the elbow of one arm with the hand of the other. Bend the knees slightly, then slowly pull your elbow behind the head while bending from the hips to the side. Hold in mild tension for 10–15 seconds. Repeat on the other side. for 10–15 seconds. Repeat on the other side.

Circulation and Legs
Lie on the floor near a wall with your lower back flat and rest your feet on the wall. This position is very relaxing, especially accompanied by slow, steady breathing, but don't overdo it. Start by holding the position for 1 minute, then gradually increase the time to 5 minutes or more.

Pilates exercises

Off-the-bike exercises form part of every Olympic cyclist's training regime. Programmes are tailored to individual needs, such as specific leg strength but nearly all, though, include elements to build core strength. These exercises can help to achieve this without the need for gym equipment.

The Hundred
Lie down with hands at your sides. Breathe in from the diaphragm and breathe out, pulling in the abdominal muscles. Bend your left leg so the thigh is at right angles to the ground and the lower leg parallel to it. Raise your right leg to the same position. Lift your head, neck and shoulders toward your legs, the eyes looking at the navel. Raise both arms and pump them up and down at your sides. Start with 10 pumps and build up to 100 pumps.
Stengthens: all abdominal muscles

Supine Unsupported Marching
Lie down as for the hundred. Once both legs are raised, lower your left leg and extend it, then lower your right leg and do the same. Repeat 10–20 times. Strengthens: the hip flexors and transverse abdominus.

Half Roll Down
Sit with knees bent at right angles, hip-width apart, feet flat on the floor. Rest your hands behind the knees, not using them to support body weight. Slowly lower your torso backward, stopping when you feel you might tip over. Hold this position for one breath, then raise the torso again. Start with 5 repetitions and build up to 10.
Strengthens: all abdominal muscles, the hip flexors and the spine.

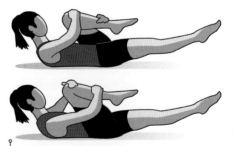

Single Leg Stretch
Lying down, lift your feet into the air with toes pointed, then raise your left knee up to your chest. Grasp the ankle with your right hand and place the left hand on the knee, breathe in and raise your shoulders off the ground, keeping your right leg sticking straight out. Breathe out and slowly switch legs. Start with 5 repetitions and build up to 10.
Strengthens: the obliques, which are on either side of the torso above the hips.

Criss-cross

Lying down with hands behind your head, raise
your knees toward your chest. Breathe in and
raise your shoulders off the ground and touch right
elbow to left knee. At the same time, extend your right
leg forward. Breathe out and switch legs, so it is left elbow
to right knee and left leg extended. Use the abdominal muscles
not the arms to raise the shoulders. Start with 5 repetitions and
build up to 10.
Strengthens: the rectus abdominus and the obliques.

Forward Plank

Lie on your stomach and prop yourself up on your elbows and
forearms with your hands flat. Straighten your legs and raise your
body so you are supported by the balls of your feet, with feet hip-
distance apart. Keep your back straight, taking care
not to arch it or stick your bottom in the air. Hold this
position for 30 seconds to begin with, extending the
time as you grow stronger.
Strengthens: lower back muscles and shoulders.

Power Bridge

Lie on your back, with arms at your side palms down.
Bend your knees and bring your heels toward your bottom.
Squeeze your bottom muscles, the glutes, and raise your
hips, pushing up from your heels, to form a straight line
from shoulders to knees. Lift your toes slightly and hold for 2
seconds. Keeping your toes raised, lower your body three-
quarters of the way down, then back up. Start with 10
repetitions and build up to 20.
Strengthens: lower back, hip flexors and glutes.

Side Plank

Lie on your right side, propped up on your elbow. Rest
left foot on top of right, raise your left arm over your
head, then push up, raising the hips so your body
forms a perfect triangle with the floor. Slowly lower
your hips toward the floor and raise them again. Do
10–15 repetitions, then repeat on the other side.
Strengthens: the transverse abdominus and obliques.

Training troubleshooting

Besides the dangers of overtraining and riding while suffering from an illness, cyclists can face problems of discomfort as well as the risk of accidents. Watch top professionals and it soon becomes apparent that even the most experienced riders fall off their bikes.

Taking a Fall

Accidents happen for all sorts of reasons, but often occur because riders are tired, overeager or inattentive, hence the need to stay alert and know your limits.

BMX and mountain bike racers are taught how to dismount off the back of the bike and it's a skill other cyclists can benefit from learning too, as it cuts the chances of getting injured. Often, however, you just don't have time to avoid a fall.

The most common injuries in cycling are skin abrasions, known as road rash, soft tissue injuries and muscular soreness. Anything more serious should be treated by a qualified first aider or doctor. The St John Ambulance Brigade are on hand at many bike races for such eventualities.

Road Rash

Road rash comes from frictional contact with the ground. The first step is to clean the wound thoroughly, removing all grit and dirt, using lots of clean water. Next apply a dressing, if necessary, to protect the wound. Dressings should be changed daily, combined with gentle cleaning with soap and water. Once a scab has formed, stop bandaging the wound, as exposing it to the air will speed the healing process.

Soft Tissue Injuries

Other soft tissue injuries such as swellings and bruising are treated with the four-step treatment RICE – Rest, Ice, Compression, Elevation.

- **Rest** – without rest, soft tissue injuries take longer to heal, can flare up and become more painful. Avoid using a damaged limb until function is restored and the pain has gone.
- **Ice** – this reduces swelling if applied as soon as possible. The classic way to do this is to wrap a packet of frozen peas in a tea towel and apply it to the affected area for 20 minutes in every hour.
- **Compression** – this can reduce further swelling, which may increase the pain and limit function. Use a snugly fitting elastic bandage over the affected area.
- **Elevation** – raising the injured limb also reduces swelling and aids the removal of waste products from the area.

Muscular Soreness

Muscular soreness, pain and stiffness may only may kick in several hours after a fall. Ibuprofen relieves the pain and it is usually best to limit activity to whatever you feel comfortable doing as this will help ease stiffness.

Staying Comfortable

Vibrations and pressure via the body's three main contact points with the bike, the saddle, handlebars and pedals can all create problems for riders.

- **Saddle:** set at the correct angle, most modern saddles are instantly comfortable. But to avoid chafing, rashes and boils, wear seamless padded cycling shorts and, for hygiene's sake, wash them and yourself after every ride.
- **Handlebars:** some riders experience loss of sensation in the hands while riding. While wearing padded gloves and using padded bar tape may resolve the problem, it's also worth checking your riding position as it may be transferring too much body weight to the hands and arms.

- **Pedals:** stiff-soled shoes are preferable to flexible ones. It is worth getting a bike shop to fit the shoe cleat for clipless pedals, which should allow some rotation of the foot. Incorrectly fitted cleats can lead to knee problems.

Cycling disciplines in detail

People of all ages can enjoy bike racing. Participation provides variety, adventure and camaraderie as well as the deep satisfaction that comes from challenging yourself and successfully rising to each challenge. So pick the branch of the sport that most appeals and have a go.

Track racing

Track Cycling is the sport's most diverse discipline with many different types of event, some requiring power and others endurance. All track racing, though, calls for great technical skills and tactical awareness.

The Events

Besides the main Olympic events of Sprint, Team Sprint, Keirin, Team Pursuit and Omnium, Track Cycling also includes other race formats: a 200-metre flying start time trial; individual pursuit; 1km and 500m time trials from a standing start; points races; the Madison (now replaced as an Olympic event by the Omnium), a relay race between teams of two riders who take turns racing, hand-slinging each other into the race; a scratch race, a massed-start race from a standing start – and an elimination race, where the last rider over the line on each lap must withdraw from the contest.

Getting Started

Find your nearest track by visiting British Cycling's website, britishcycling.org.uk. While velodromes are the main focus of Track racing, racing on grass tracks also takes place around the country and is well worth having a go. Most hard-surface tracks have resident clubs that offer taster sessions where you can learn the basic skills from a qualified coach and many also have bikes for hire at reasonable cost.

Under-16s should seek out a Go-Ride accredited club (see page 18) that offers sessions teaching the basic skills needed for Track riding. All under-18s will need permission from their parents or guardian to take part.

To race, you will need to be a member of British Cycling and hold a racing licence (see pages 18–19).

Gear

Helmets are compulsory on the track and padded fingerless gloves are strongly recommended. Otherwise, for novices, any long-sleeved, tight-fitting top and tight-fitting shorts or trousers, preferably not jeans or anything with a prominent seam in the groin, will be suitable.

Competitive Cycling

Track leagues: most new riders start out racing in their local track league, a regular series of meetings throughout the summer, and in winter at indoor velodromes. Competitors win points based on their results at each meeting that determine overall position at the end of the series. Entry requirements for participation in leagues vary, so check with the organisers in advance.

Series: a number of series are held in summer that bring together specialists such as sprinters and omnium riders at meetings around the country. Points are awarded at each round that determine the overall series winners.

One-off meetings: anyone with the appropriate racing licence can enter an open meeting, while invitation meetings are reserved for elite riders.

Championships: some British Cycling regions hold regional championships, and the British Cycling National Championships are spread around the country. Specific events, such as the Omnium, Madison and Tandem Sprint, have their own title meetings. The main focus, though, is on the annual British Cycling Track Championships where senior men and women compete in the most popular disciplines.

The competitive careers of most Olympic Track specialists began at their local track league.

The velodrome

Tracks come in all shapes and sizes, from municipal outdoor ones to state-of-the-art velodromes built for international events. Every track carries markings to ensure fair competition and understanding what they mean is essential for riders and spectators alike.

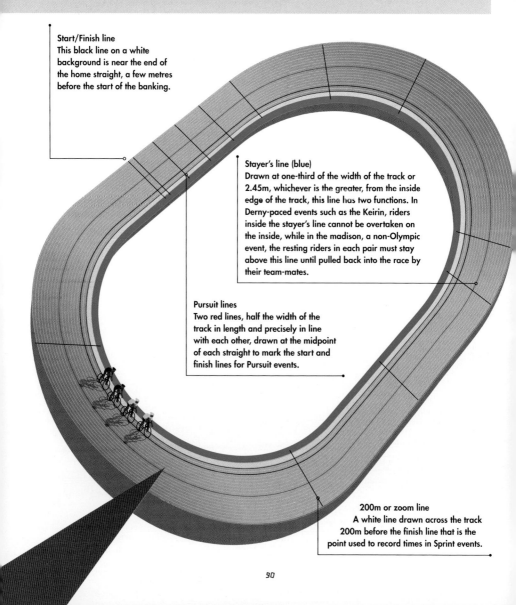

Start/Finish line
This black line on a white background is near the end of the home straight, a few metres before the start of the banking.

Stayer's line (blue)
Drawn at one-third of the width of the track or 2.45m, whichever is the greater, from the inside edge of the track, this line has two functions. In Derny-paced events such as the Keirin, riders inside the stayer's line cannot be overtaken on the inside, while in the madison, a non-Olympic event, the resting riders in each pair must stay above this line until pulled back into the race by their team-mates.

Pursuit lines
Two red lines, half the width of the track in length and precisely in line with each other, drawn at the midpoint of each straight to mark the start and finish lines for Pursuit events.

200m or zoom line
A white line drawn across the track 200m before the finish line that is the point used to record times in Sprint events.

Sprinter's line (red)
This is marked out 85cm from the track's inside edge. The space between the pole and sprinter's lines is the fastest route round the track and any rider in it cannot be overtaken on the inside.

Track surface
The London 2012 Velodrome track is surfaced with 40-millimetre square, 6m long lathes of Siberian larch, a sustainably sourced softwood.

Gauge line or datum line (black)
Painted 20 centimetres from the inside of the track, this line is the official measure of the track's length.

Blue band or Côte d'Azur (pale blue)
A rideable surface that runs at the base of the track. Riders can use it for training but must not stray on to it in a race except in an emergency.

London 2012 Velodrome

A cycling track has to be symmetrical and contain two straights and two turns. In addition, for Olympic and World Championship competition it has to be 250m long and at least 7m wide. All track designers, including the design team behind the London 2012 Velodrome, want to build a track that's fast.

A fast track is one that lets a rider travel at maximum speed with minimum effort. Long flat straights with two banked turns don't fit these requirements. Instead, engineers and designers have used computers to create a track geometry that does: short straights banked at about 10 degrees, transitional curves with steadily increasing banking angles leading into circular curves banked at about 45 degrees, then transitional curves featuring different angles that lead back into the straights. Air temperature is also controlled to ensure the track is fast.

The Velodrome is Britain's fourth indoor track; the others are in Manchester, Calshot near Southampton and Newport, South Wales. A further 18 outdoor tracks operate around the country, varying in length from 150m to 500m and mostly with concrete, asphalt or tarmac surfaces. To find their locations, visit britishcycling.org.uk.

Track training tips and tactics

Ride regularly at your local track to become familiar with the dynamics and quirks of the track, riding in a fast-moving group and the strengths and weaknesses of other local track regulars.

Bike Control

Before venturing on to the track, first learn to slow down and stop by applying pressure backward on the pedals to reduce speed gradually. Because you can't freewheel, you have to get accustomed to your legs being in constant motion – it's important you turn the pedals rather than they turn your legs.

Because the bike has a fixed gear, actions as apparently simple as changing body and hand position require practice too. With events that begin from a standing start, such as the pursuit, it is important to be able to accelerate out of the saddle, then get into an aerodynamic riding position as quickly and smoothly as possible.

Joining the Track

Learn how to get on and off the track from both the outside perimeter rail and the inside of the track – it is important to be able to safely join the track, maintain a straight line on starting and gain speed with confidence. Similarly, you must be able to leave the track and stop at the rail or in the centre without impeding others.

Starting on the inner edge of the track, practise riding in a straight line and cornering while pedalling, following the natural line of the track. Once you are confident with this, you can start to

venture further up the banking, always avoiding sudden changes of direction. The banking on outdoor tracks is less steep than indoor velodromes so is less daunting for beginners.

Riding in a Group

Some events can have as many as 40 riders taking part, so you have to be comfortable with leading other riders, following a wheel without overlapping and riding side by side. Vigilance is key – you have to be aware of what is happening all round you and not do anything erratic like make sudden changes of direction or speed.

Follow the Leader is a fun drill that many coaches use. It takes riders all over the track, teaching them not only how to follow a wheel but also the importance of maintaining a steady pace, so that the line is evenly spread out.

Use a Coach

A qualified coach is on hand at most track training sessions. They can advise on how to develop the high-cadence pedalling at the core of track cycling and boost your skill levels in other departments.

Race Training

Track riders divide their time between the track, the road and the gym, combining these three elements to produce the mix of speed, endurance and technique that track racing demands.

Away from the track, training involves the same mixture of basic endurance fitness gained from steady, easy rides and shorter high-intensity interval training rides as time trialling and road racing, although it isn't necessary to put in the same long hours in the saddle required for the latter.

Gym work is important for body conditioning, and, particularly for sprinters, in order to build the muscle mass required for explosive efforts. Every rider is different and has different goals, so a coach will recommend a programme of gym exercises and weight training to suit you and what you want to achieve.

A Derny rider leads racing cyclists around the track in the Keirin event.

The track stand

Casual observers are often baffled to see sprint cyclists standing still, failing to understand that it's a way to try and force a rival rider to lose tactical advantage by taking the lead. In fact, the ability to do a track stand is a useful technique for any rider to acquire.

Find a quiet spot, on grass or tarmac, preferably with a slight incline. Start out with your feet unclipped from the pedals and, if you are on a road bike, the bike in a middle gear. Ride slowly out of the saddle and when the crankarms are parallel to the ground and your stronger foot is forward, come to a stop, turning the front wheel slightly uphill.

Apply gentle pressure on the forward pedal while simultaneously counteracting this forward force by feathering the brakes: use small amounts of pedal pressure to ride a tiny bit forward, a tiny bit back by ratcheting the pedals back and forth, keeping the crankarms parallel.

At the same time, turn the handlebars slightly left and right to maintain balance. Any movement of pedals and handlebars should be minute.

Track techniques explained

Once track riding becomes second nature, it benefits riding technique in other cycling disciplines by helping to develop a higher cadence and a smooth constant supply of power to the pedals.

Track Skills

Once the basics of riding safely and confidently on the track are in place, tactical awareness is the next skill to develop. Often you can identify a strong competitor before the start of the race. Treat them as targets and shadow them by hanging just behind and above them, so you can react if they make a move. The aim is to conserve energy until the time is right to launch an attack.

The Start

Track racing has two ways to start depending on the event: a held start, where a helper holds the bike and rider from the side; and a standing start where a helper holds the bike from behind. In either instance, you need to set off with your stronger foot on the forward pedal, which is set at the 'two o'clock' position to allow maximum pressure on the first pedal stroke.

Overtaking

You can't overtake on the inside, only above a rider, so you have to make sure the way is clear behind before making your move, choose a line that's a safe distance away from the rider you are overtaking and only come back down on to the line when your back wheel is well clear of the passed rider.

Joining In

Joining and leaving a line, usually moving off the front of the group and rejoining it at its tail, is another basic track technique. Be aware of overtaking

Sir Chris Hoy

The Scot's love affair with cycling began with BMX at the age of seven and by the time he was in his teens he was one of the world's 10 best riders. Since turning his attention to the track, he has won medals in every World Championship from 1999 to 2010. His first Olympic gold came at the Athens 2004 Olympic Games with victory in the 1km Individual Time Trial. Winning the Team Sprint gold with Jason Kenny and Jamie Staff, then following it with solo victories in the Keirin and the Individual Sprint at Beijing 2008, Hoy became a national hero as the first Briton in 100 years to win three gold medals at a single Games.

riders, then signal verbally and with a gesture to those behind you in the line that you are about to move out of it and accelerate up the track above the stayer's line to leave the group. When rejoining the line, mark the position of the last rider and be travelling at sufficient speed to then drop down, using the bank to aid acceleration, and slot in behind. A good transition is a smooth one where you are not left scrambling to get back in the line.

Technique Tip
On the track, the banking has a noticeable impact on speed. The higher up you ride, the slower you get. Conversely, riders can gain speed when they descend the bank, a tactic widely used in sprint competitions. Much depends on the angle you use to climb and descend the banking – a gradual ascent, for example, makes it easier to maintain speed than a steep one.

The lead rider leaves a line. He pulls out, lets the other riders through, then rejoins at the back of the group.

Road racing

Road racing is cycling's best-known discipline, with a long history rich in epic battles and outstanding winners. Its first past the post principle may sound straightforward, but riders require great endurance, power and tactical awareness just to be in contention for victory.

The Event

Road racing is massed-start racing that takes place on public roads or tarmac circuits during a season that runs from March to October. One-day races range in distance from less than 20km for under-16s to more than 200km for elite racers, and attract from 20 to 200 competitors depending on the event. Races are categorised by age and ability, so if you are new to the sport you will not find yourself lined up against hardened professionals.

Contested on purpose-built tarmac circuits or tracks shared with other sports such as motor racing and go-karting, circuit races are an ideal, traffic-free introduction to road racing. Meetings, often held on midweek evenings, cater for a variety of abilities and age groups. With laps ranging from 1km to 4km and races lasting anything from 20 minutes to an hour, they are a great way to hone your riding skills and gain an understanding of the tactical subtleties of the sport.

Getting Started

To get involved in road racing, it's a good idea to join a club. Club training rides are a great way to get fit and learn how to ride in a group, an essential skill in road racing. Most

Lance Armstrong

Armstrong's prodigious talent showed early when he won the US amateur road race championship in 1991 and became world champion two years later at the age of 21. But in 1996, just as his professional career was taking off, he was diagnosed with testicular cancer, the disease spreading to his lungs, abdomen and brain. Remarkably, after surgery and chemotherapy, he was back in training by 1998 and focused on one prize: the Tour de France. A record seven victories in that race between 1999 and 2005 and his tireless campaigning for Livestrong and the Lance Armstrong Foundation, now one of America's biggest funders of cancer research, have made him a hero to millions of people around the world.

Endurance, power, mental determination and tactical awareness are important road racing traits.

clubs have a longer run on Sundays and one or two shorter evening runs during the week. Other club members will be able to point you in the direction of suitable races for beginners and explain how to enter them.

To race, you will need to be a member of British Cycling and hold a racing licence (see pages 18–19). Check the British Cycling website for details of races in your area. Some accept entries on the

line; others have a cut-off date for entries usually three weeks before the race.

As well as the essentials of pedalling, correct gear usage, braking, descending, climbing and cornering, road racers need to be able to take on food and drink from helpers at the roadside and eat and drink safely on the bike.

Races on open roads

Races held on public roads are longer and offer more varied terrain than circuit racing, which usually means the main pack of riders, or peloton, takes on a more fluid shape as riders seek to conserve energy by sheltering behind other riders.

Race Organisation

Closing roads in Britain is more complicated than elsewhere in Europe and is heavily dependent on police consent, so few race organisers close the entire route of their race. Instead, they use a rolling road closure, with marshals, motorbike escorts and official cars blocking just the portion of road immediately around the field of riders.

Riders have to be aware of oncoming traffic and other potential hazards such

Team cars
Each one usually contains the team director and a mechanic. It is stocked up with spare bikes and wheels, food and water and a radio linked both to the race radio and to its riders. With the race director's permission, cars can move up to the bunch when required. Domestiques also go back to the team car to collect supplies for their team-mates.

Lead motorcycle
Travels just ahead of the lead riders to ensure the route is clear and to alert spectators that the cyclists are coming.

as pedestrians and parked cars. Safety is always the priority for race organisers and riders alike.

On the Continent, complete road closures are much more common. Because of its size and prestige, the Tour de France has the most sophisticated race organisation, coordinating the movements of a small army of team and race officials, press and publicists.

A Team Effort

For the professionals in particular, cycling is a team sport. Squads bring together riders with different specialities: a team leader who has the tactical awareness and ability to win big races; small, wiry climbers to excel in the mountains; a time triallist for the big tours, which always feature a race against the clock; a sprint specialist with the power to accelerate fast to snatch victory by inches in bunch sprints; and 'domestiques', workhorse riders who chase down rivals, protect their team leaders and fetch and carry for the team's benefit.

The riders
They may be together in a bunch or split into several different groups depending on the terrain, the weather or tactics.

Race director's car
The nerve centre of the race follows just behind the lead riders, keeping track of the action and via radio relaying information and issuing orders to all motorcycles and cars following the race.

Road racing techniques and tactics

Once you have confidence in your fitness, basic bike handling skills and ability to ride in a group, it's time to think about road racing techniques and tactics.

The Start

To accelerate quickly from the line, start off in an easier gear than you anticipate using for most of the race.

Breakaways

Although a group of riders moves more quickly than a lone cyclist, it doesn't stop riders from attacking. They may see a rival is not in a position to react, or feel geographical features such as a hill or corner may help them escape successfully. Most riders make their move from three or four places back in the bunch, accelerating hard to gain a decisive gap, and must be exceptionally strong to stay out in front for any length of time.

A breakaway's chances of survival increase if it includes more than one rider, because it is less tiring when more people share the pace. So while one rider might initiate the break, other riders may take the opportunity to join it, reckoning on a better chance of success in a small group of rivals than in a much larger bunch sprint.

To increase the pace and reel in a breakaway, the main group has to cooperate, especially as a small breakaway group poses a greater threat to the race's final outcome than a lone cyclist. Once a break is reeled in, however, another enterprising rider or group of riders may choose that moment to launch another breakaway attack.

Wind Tactics

Road riders do all they can to shelter from the wind to conserve energy.

Single line: in a single line, one rider takes the brunt of the wind and the others tuck in behind. After 20–30

Bunch sprint 1
Leading up to the final sprint, the sheltered riders in yellow are in the ideal attack position. The blue riders are positioned too far back.

Bunch sprint 2
The yellow and red riders push onto the finish in the final surge and the badly positioned blues are left trailing.

seconds, the lead rider moves off the front on the windward side of the group, sheltering other riders and drifting to the back of the line, while the next rider moves forward to take a turn at the front.

Through and off: in this formation, two lead riders at the front are followed by two parallel lines of riders. The leaders move back as above, then start moving forward again for their next turn at the front. In effect, it's a conveyor belt of riders, moving down one line to provide shelter and up the other while protected from the wind.

Echelon: it the wind hits a group at an angle, riders spread across the road to form an echelon. The rider at the windward end of the formation briefly takes the brunt of the wind's force, then drifts back and across to take up position at the most sheltered end.

Towards the Finish

As the race reaches its decisive phase, it's important to be well-placed in a group and alert to any signs of an attack. Look out for gaps in the group and avoid being boxed in by other riders. Follow in the slipstream of other riders and hold your position firmly. If someone overtakes while you are behind one rider, try to follow their wheel instead.

In a small group, try to let others take the lead, so you can jump past them at the last second. The big high-intensity effort comes in the last 120–160m, but aim for a point 10m or so beyond that so you hit the line at top speed. Once you've crossed the line, don't brake suddenly or following riders will pile into the back of you.

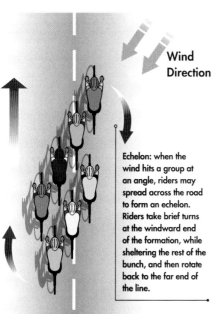

Wind Direction

Echelon: when the wind hits a group at an angle, riders may spread across the road to form an echelon. Riders take brief turns at the windward end of the formation, while sheltering the rest of the bunch, and then rotate back to the far end of the line.

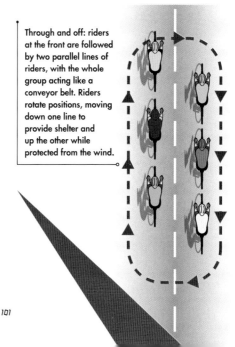

Through and off: riders at the front are followed by two parallel lines of riders, with the whole group acting like a conveyor belt. Riders rotate positions, moving down one line to provide shelter and up the other while protected from the wind.

Time trialling

The time trial is one of cycling's most easily understood events, a race not only against the clock but also against yourself. Because every rider wants to go faster and every time trial shows whether they have, it can become addictive.

The Event

Time trialling takes place on open roads, usually early in the morning or early in the evening, with riders setting off at one-minute intervals and seeing how fast they can complete a set distance. Most courses are either 'out and back', often turning at a roundabout, or loops based on left-hand turns to avoid crossing traffic.

The most common time trial distances in Britain are 10, 25, 50 and 100 miles. For experienced riders, there are also 12-hour and 24-hour time trials. Clubs organise time trials over other distances, as well as 'sporting' time trials, usually over hillier courses and, particularly in autumn, hill climbs. The majority of time trials are for solo riders, but there are also events for two-up, three-up and four-up teams.

Getting Started

If you can ride a bike in traffic, you can have a go at riding a time trial. The only stipulation is that you must wear a helmet and be over 12 years of age and, if you are under 18 years old, you must have a signed consent form from your parents or guardian. Any kind of bike, apart from recumbents, is permitted.

Many clubs run 'Come and Try It' events open to anyone who fancies having a go at time trialling. After testing

Eddy Merckx

The Belgian nicknamed 'the Cannibal' was formidable in all departments, winning five Tours de France and dominating the 1969 race so completely that he became the only cyclist to win the yellow, green and red polka-dot jerseys in the same Tour. Merckx sealed his reputation against the clock in October 1972 when he set a new world hour record of 49.431 kilometres in Mexico City, a record that stood for 12 years. Merckx's bike for that ride looks surprisingly ordinary compared to today's aerodynamic machines and is now on display in the Brussels metro station named in his honour.

the water, joining a Cycling Time Trials (CTT) affiliated club is the next step (see page 19). Most clubs organise informal time trials open to members of any CTT-affiliated club. Newcomers to the sport usually start with 10-mile time trials and move up to longer distances as their fitness improves and their experience grows.

Competitive Cycling

Association events: entry for these races is limited to members of clubs affiliated to their local regional association. This promotes friendly rivalry and also gives more riders access to courses that are fast, because open events on such courses are often oversubscribed.

Open events: these usually take place at weekends and some are so popular that competitors are selected on past results.

Season-long competitions: top time triallists compete for annual Best British All-Rounder titles based on the fastest average speed over their category distances. CTT also runs the season-long Road Time Trial Council (RTTC) and Time Trial (TT) series based on hilly or sporting courses. Riders are awarded points based on their results, which determine the series winner.

National championships: riders under the age of 17 can compete for the George Herbert Stancer Trophy, a schools-based competition. National championships are held for each category and British Cycling and CTT jointly promote a British Time Trial Championship.

Time triallists accelerate out of the saddle away from the start, then drop into a more aerodynamic position.

Time trial techniques and training

Maintaining a high speed consistently requires self-awareness, self-control and patience, because it takes time to bring out the best in yourself. Good riding skills are needed, too, since riding the wrong line can cost precious seconds.

Time Trial Skills

Once they have accelerated away from the start, successful time triallists are able to move smoothly into the most aerodynamic position possible. While riding, they are alert to other traffic and keep a constant eye on the road ahead so they can safely negotiate changes of road surface, avoid potholes and other obstacles and stay on course.

The Start

A helper holds the bike upright at the start of a time trial, so you need to be used to being held in this way. You must also be in the correct gear for starting, usually two or three sprockets lower than the main gear you intend to use for the time trial.

In time trialling it is important for riders to pace themselves and ride close to their anaerobic threshold.

Target Times

Your first time trial result automatically sets your own personal best, a set of figures you will want to beat next time. Otherwise, the classic targets for average club time triallists are 25 minutes for a 10-mile event and under an hour for a 25-mile time trial.

Training

Time trialling is all about pacing yourself, riding at close to your anaerobic threshold throughout the event. Go over the limit and you will blow up, stay too far under it and your speed will drop. Race distance dictates the level of effort required, too. Short time trials can be ridden at closer to anaerobic threshold than longer ones.

Learning to ride at high cadence and high intensity takes time. Training with a heart rate monitor is the easiest way to see how close you are to your anaerobic threshold, although you also must also pay attention to what your body tells you and be careful not to overdo it.

Most time triallists spend the winter months building a good endurance base by riding steady, low-intensity miles, then in spring start adding one or two short training rides a week that feature short intervals at racing intensity. Gradually over the weeks the frequency and length of these sprints are built up until riders can sustain high speeds for the duration of their target time trial. In summer, racing time trials often provides all the speed training necessary.

A Little History

All courses in the *Cycling Time Trails Handbook* carry a code, such as G25/53. The course code begins with a letter to identify the region, in this case G for London South, usually followed by a distance, such as 25, then a number for the course's exact location.

This system is a throwback to before the Second World War when bike racing was made illegal in Britain. Competitors turned to time trialling to get round the ban; with cyclists riding on their own it was hard for the police to tell if they were racing. Coding courses was designed to throw the authorities off the scent and has remained in use today, although the CTT Handbook and website now give details of every route!

How to Enter an Open Event

To find out where open events are taking place and where to post entries, you will need a CTT Handbook, which you can order online from cyclingtimetrials.org.uk. To enter, you must be a member of a CTT-affiliated club and register in advance by post using a standard entry form available from the CTT website or your club secretary. Once your entry has been accepted, you will receive a start sheet before the event giving course details and your starting time. After the race the organisers will post you a result sheet with your official time.

Mountain biking

Mountain Biking, like BMX, is one of the newest Olympic disciplines, riding its way into the Games on the back of its huge popularity worldwide. It's easy to see the appeal – no two off-road trails are ever the same, making racing fun, full of variety and endlessly challenging.

The Events

Cross-country is the Olympic form of the sport, a first past the post race held on circuits of between 4 and 9km that offer plenty of climbing and descending, technical sections, jumps, drop-offs and varied terrain. Senior races entail multiple laps of the circuit and last 1.5–2 hours.

Other forms of cross-country racing include marathons, which are longer races on longer circuits; enduros, in which individuals or teams of riders see how far they can ride in a set time period; and short-track, held on shorter circuits and lasting less time than a standard cross-country event.

The main other mountain bike events are four-cross – a short 300–600m downhill course full of obstacles and corners that is contested by four riders at a time with the fastest from each heat going through to the next round; and downhill – an individual time trial descent over varied terrain.

Getting Started

You don't have to join a club in order to race, but it is highly recommended. Some clubs are dedicated solely to mountain

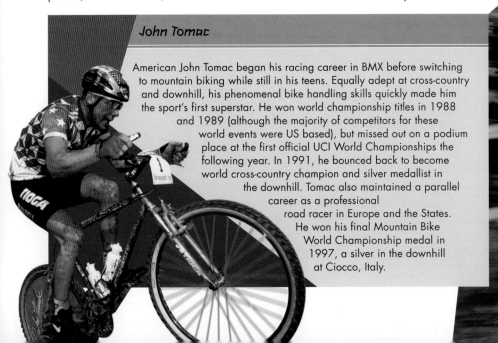

John Tomac

American John Tomac began his racing career in BMX before switching to mountain biking while still in his teens. Equally adept at cross-country and downhill, his phenomenal bike handling skills quickly made him the sport's first superstar. He won world championship titles in 1988 and 1989 (although the majority of competitors for these world events were US based), but missed out on a podium place at the first official UCI World Championships the following year. In 1991, he bounced back to become world cross-country champion and silver medallist in the downhill. Tomac also maintained a parallel career as a professional road racer in Europe and the States. He won his final Mountain Bike World Championship medal in 1997, a silver in the downhill at Ciocco, Italy.

biking, which means other club members are likely to know good places to ride.

Riders are categorised by age – from under-12 to Super Veteran for over 60s – and ability, which ranges from fun to elite. For under-16s, Go-Ride Racing (see page 18) offers an opportunity to learn the skills from a qualified coach and have a go at racing in events that last from 10 to 30 minutes depending on the rider's age.

You do not need a racing licence to compete in local events, but to gain points for the national ranking system you will need to be a member of British Cycling and have a racing licence.

Gear

Helmets are compulsory in races, and gloves and eye protection are strongly advised. Pay particular attention to footwear. Mountain bikers often spend time pushing their bikes or getting their feet wet riding through streams and puddles, so you need shoes that have good grip and offer a degree of protection from water. Otherwise, clothing should be tight-fitting and not have seams in awkward places that will chafe and rub.

Ever challenging and full of variety, Mountain Biking is contested over a range of distances.

Mountain bike techniques explained

Don't neglect the basics of braking, climbing, descending, cornering, pedalling and gear use described elsewhere in this book. When you go for a ride, don't initially try to get them all right all at once.

Attack Position

The Start

Competitors must start with one foot on the ground, so practise getting that foot to the pedal as quickly and smoothly as possible. Arrive at the start line with the bike in a gear that will allow you to make a quick acceleration out of the saddle away from the line when the signal is given.

Momentum

Every rider at some stage has started climbing a steep bank only to discover they didn't hit it fast enough or in the right gear and as a result have come to a slow, agonising halt that's forced them to dismount hastily and push the bike to the top. They have lost momentum, the force that keeps things moving. Because the terrain is tougher and more varied off-road, maintaining momentum matters more in mountain biking than in any other branch of cycling.

Attack Position

This position lets you be ready for anything the trail may throw at you. Stand on the pedals with the crankarms horizontal, knees slightly bent, weight over the bottom bracket, hands covering the brakes and head up so you can see what's coming next. Keep your body relaxed, using the arms and legs as shock

absorbers to soak up the rough stuff.

In this position the bike can move underneath you while you retain control of it through your hands and feet. From it, your body can move backward on descents or forward on climbs, all the time keeping the weight over the bottom bracket. Shifting weight for balance and allowing the bike to move are at the heart of mountain bike technique.

Manual Front Wheel Lift

To clear obstacles, start in the attack position, rock forward as you near the obstacle, then quickly shift your body weight backward, pulling up with the shoulders and lower back to lift the front wheel.

Power-assisted Front Wheel Lift

With your weight back on the saddle, have your stronger foot on the pedal in

Front
Wheel Lift

Step-overs and Step-ups

By combining front and rear wheel lifts in one fluid action, riders can clear an obstacle – a technique known as a step-over – or climb stepped sections, a step-up.

Manual Drop-offs

To negotiate a small but steep drop from one section of a trail to a lower level, start in the attack position and lift the front wheel just before the edge of the drop. Shift your body weight so it returns to above the bottom bracket as the rear wheel hits the edge. The aim is to land both wheels simultaneously, using the arms and legs to absorb the impact

the two o'clock position and, just as you near the obstacle, push down hard on it, while pulling up on the bars using the shoulders and lower back, keeping the arms straight, to lift the wheel.

Rear Wheel Lift

Once the front end has cleared an obstacle, the rear wheel needs to follow suit. From the attack position, throw your body weight forward and up, while pushing back on the pedals with toes pointing down and scooping the feet up on the pedals.

Track Stand

This is useful for understanding balance and for tackling low-speed technical sections. See page 93 for a how-to guide.

Pumping and Bunny-hops

Both are important techniques in Mountain Biking. See pages 117 and 119 for how-to guides.

Ascending

Descending

Mountain bike training

Whether you are training or just riding for fun, whenever you venture off-road, respect for the environment and for other trail users is essential and, for safety's sake, it is vital that you are prepared for all eventualities too.

Where to Ride

Races take place in public parks, private estates and on Forestry Commission land, always with the landowners' consent. When you are training or just going for a ride, you can cycle legally on bridleways, byways, green lanes and waymarked cycle routes on Forestry Commission land. Many of these are shared with walkers and horse riders so slow down and be courteous when necessary. Cycling on footpaths and canal towpaths is illegal.

Safety

On all rides take sufficient food and water, a basic toolkit for emergency repairs and a mobile phone. Whenever you go off-road, let someone know where you are going and when you expect to be back, so they can raise the alarm if you don't return.

Most accidents happen because riders lose concentration or lack sufficient skills to handle the terrain. Know your limits and extend them gradually. If you have just mastered a small drop-off, for instance, progress to slightly steeper ones rather than assume you are now ready for a severe drop.

Be aware, too, that weather conditions have a big impact on mountain bike handling. A trail with lots of tree roots may present few hazards on a hot, sunny day; when it is wet the roots can become slippery and treacherous, so practise in all conditions.

Training

Because mountain biking is so technically demanding, first concentrate on building your skills gradually. Once confident you can instinctively handle most obstacles, you can then work on developing endurance, strength and power. Consult a coach to determine the best training regime for you and remember to allow plenty of recovery time between rides.

Very few top riders rely solely on mountain biking for training. Most ride the road for the steady, low-intensity miles that build endurance and do gym work to boost strength, muscle power and flexibility. Sustained power is important in a mountain bike race, because riders gain no aerodynamic advantage from being in a bunch and have to keep the wheels turning to maintain momentum. Short, higher-intensity training rides, on- or off-road, are used to lift the lactate threshold, allowing riders to make a quick start and ride harder for longer.

Mountain bike trails can provide many hazards so good concentration is essential.

Competitive cycling

Many race meetings are two-day weekend events that cater for all levels of ability. British Cycling divides races into six categories and provides a comprehensive racing calendar on its website. If you hold a racing licence, national ranking points can be gained in all categories apart from Regional B.

Regional B: local grassroots racing that provides an informal introduction to the sport.

Regional A: regional series events that are open to anyone but the majority of competitors are from local clubs.

National B: regional championships and the British Cycling national points series, which features talented racers in the main categories and also has less serious races for fun category and younger riders.

National A: the British Cycling National Championships.

International B: the UCI World Cup series, which is primarily for elite riders.

International A: the Olympic Games and the UCI World Championships.

BMX

Fun, competitive yet informal, BMX is where many people first fall in love with cycling. With racing open to all, from novice to expert, and for all ages, it's the perfect introduction to the sport.

Getting Started

The governing body for BMX is British Cycling and you can find details of local clubs and tracks through its website, britishcycling.org.uk. Under-16s should look for Go-Ride accredited clubs as they are geared specifically towards introducing young people to the sport. The racing season runs from April through to September, with club race and training evenings held every week, though some clubs also organise winter events. You do not need a racing licence to compete in club races, but BMX national events do require a licence (see pages 18–19).

Although BMX experts use specialised racing bikes, any BMX bike will do for novices. The only stipulations are that the bike should be in good mechanical repair with a working brake and adequate tread on the tyres. The handlebar grips must not be torn or expose the end of the bars and the bike must have no pegs or chainguard fitted.

BMX calls for endurance, strength, speed, and excellent bike handling skills.

Shanaze Reade

At the age of 10, Reade began racing at her local track in Crewe and the first BMX she owned was bought for £1. A phenomenally powerful rider, she has won one junior and three elite women's world championships, as well as a cabinetful of British and European titles.

Such is her strength that in 2006, at the age of 17, she raced the British National series against the men and won to became British National No.1 in the '19 and over' elite men's category. The only accolade to elude her so far is an Olympic medal – a crash in the final at the 2008 Beijing Games took her out of contention.

Reade has also proved a formidable track cyclist. In only her second track race, she teamed up with Victoria Pendleton to win gold in the Team Sprint at the 2007 World Track Championships.

Gear

A helmet is required, though many clubs will lend one of these to novices. Full-finger gloves are also compulsory. Otherwise, a loose-fitting, long-sleeved shirt, loose-fitting long trousers or jeans and flat soled skateboard or tennis shoes are recommended. Many riders wear elbow and knee pads and other pieces of body armour.

Technique Tips

Learn to handle small jumps with complete confidence before moving on to more ambitious ones. Practice makes perfect; wreckless makes wrecks, so don't be impatient. Be progressive, graduating from one skill level to the next.

The BMX track

BMX tracks are designed to challenge a rider's skills, athleticism and nerve by cramming in a wide variety of jumps and technical sections in a compact space. Every track builder's goal is to produce a circuit where high-speed thrills are guaranteed for riders and spectators alike.

Olympic Tracks

An Olympic-standard BMX track differs from most other tracks because it is designed to include more challenging, alternative sections to be used only for top-level competition, including the battle for medals at the Olympic Games. BMX tracks are compact, closed looped designs, and the rules for Olympic competition state that they must be between 300m and 400m in length and at least 10m wide at the start and no narrower than 5m wide at any point on the course.

Most BMX tracks in Britain are made by moving earth to form the basic outline and contours. Berms (the raised walls around the outside of corners) are usually made of asphalt, which keeps its shape and provides good grip, with the rest of the course covered in a fine limestone powder that provides a more forgiving surface to land on when riders fall.

Step-ups
These have a take-off and flat section, like a tabletop, but with an additional hump before the landing begins. Riders can either jump straight from the first take-off to the landing or ride up the first take-off and then jump from the second hump.

Step-downs
A step-up in reverse, with two possible landings. Most riders will aim to jump for the second landing.

Small doubles, big doubles,
pro doubles, small triples
Put two or three speed jumps together in
close proximity and you have a double or
triple. These vary considerably in size and
offer riders the option of jumping them or
manualling through them.

Starting hill
The starting ramp for Olympic competition, a
temporary structure, must be at least 8m above
the grade of the first straight, with the initial incline
from the starting gate a minimum 12m long. On the
hill itself, there's a textured start pad, where riders
line up for the off, and the starting gate, which is
electronically or electro-pneumatically operated.

Tabletops
With a flat section between take-off and
landing, tabletops are ideal sections for
beginners to hone their jumping skills
because any rider who doesn't have
enough speed or elevation to clear the
distance can still land safely.

Rhythm section
Combining a variety of different jumps
in close proximity, rhythm sections are
designed to test riders' bike handling
skills and in particular their ability to
maintain momentum through a section
where they have no opportunity to pedal.

Rollers or speed jumps
Known either as a roller or a
speed jump, this is the basic
technical obstacle on a course, a
single rounded jump, usually less
than 1m high. Riders generally
pedal them or lift their front wheel
over the apex of the bump.

BMX track techniques and training

BMX calls for endurance, strength, power, speed, flexibility, excellent bike handling skills and a smooth, flowing riding style. Racing techniques can be gradually improved on the track, where you will also learn to engage all your senses to be alert to other riders and what obstacle is coming next.

The Start

Races are often won or lost right at the start, so most BMX tracks run specific training sessions for the starting gate. Be sure to attend these as you need to get used to balancing on the bike, with pedals level and your strong foot forward, and the front wheel pressed against the gate.

Away from the track, you can practise by pressing the front wheel up against a wall or other solid object to see how long you can hold the balance. It's much easier to do this if you look straight ahead and bend your legs slightly while keeping your arms straight.

Quick Getaway

Once the gate drops, it's time to accelerate as fast as possible. Practise standing on the pedals, arms extended but slightly bent, pushing down hard on the pedals while simultaneously pulling up on the bars.

Work to develop pedalling smoothly at high cadence by sprinting at maximum speed over a set distance. Find somewhere flat, measure out a 50-metre stretch and from a standing start go flat out over the distance. This will take it out of you, so allow four to five minutes to recover before having another go – and don't do more than two or three sprints in one session.

Braking

Use the single brake for controlled slowing down rather than stopping. To do this successfully, hands must grip the bars firmly and enough body weight must be over the rear wheel for good traction. Jamming the brake on too hard makes the bike skid, which damages tyres and, when other riders are very close, may damage you too.

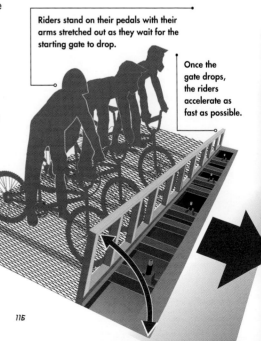

Riders stand on their pedals with their arms stretched out as they wait for the starting gate to drop.

Once the gate drops, the riders accelerate as fast as possible.

Pumping

Every track has sections where you need to maintain momentum. A smooth, flowing riding style uses weight shifting and the shock-absorbing qualities of the arms and legs to handle these sections.

As you approach the start of a roller, pull the handlebars toward you to take weight off the front wheel. As the wheel goes over the top, you don't want it to take off, so push down and forward on the bars to keep contact with the ground. When the rear wheel reaches the top, push down hard with your legs to maintain speed.

Dismounting

For safe dismounting, while pedalling shift your body weight backward and at the same time pull up on the bars to lift the front wheel. As the bike comes past the balancing point, hop off the back, keeping a grip on the bars and making sure the back wheel doesn't overtake the front one.

Cornering

Good cornering skills are important on the track, because with the right line you can overtake rivals. Practise following different lines with friends, so you get used to the possibilities. The classic tactic is to swoop wide at the start of the turn, using the berm to gain speed, then pass inside as you exit the corner. But you can also take the inside line and take the exit wide, cutting off the options for a rider who has gone wider on the berm.

The rider in red uses two different lines to overtake on a corner, going wide, *pictured left*, and cutting inside, *pictured right*. In both cases, the manoeuvre blocks a rival's exit line.

BMX Jump Techniques and Training

Training regularly at a track gives you access to coaching and the experience of other riders, who can offer advice and encouragement and teach you how to nail techniques that you may be finding difficult. To practise many of the basics, though, a decent-sized patch of grass or tarmac and the right protective gear is all you need.

Wheelies

These are all about balance and how a shift in body weight changes the bike's balance point. While pedalling, lean forward at the waist and bend your arms and knees. Then, in a single movement, throw your weight back while straightening your arms to pull the front wheel off the ground. Your body weight should be over the bike's rear wheel. Start out by trying wheelies sitting down and once you have mastered that try them standing up. If the front wheel drops, shift your weight a bit further back. If it comes up too high, bring it down by applying the brake.

Manuals

An important technique to master for jumps and technical sections, this is essentially a wheelie executed while freewheeling rather than pedalling. The main difference is that you start with the pedals parallel to the ground and, shifting your body weight backward, you lift the front wheel. It's important, though, not to lock the legs as you need them to act as shock absorbers when you return to two wheels.

Bunny-hops

Lifting both wheels off the ground is another key skill for jumps. Start by trying to clear small obstacles, preferably something that will give if you land on it, such as a plastic bottle. Approach the obstacle slowly, with the pedals parallel to the ground, crouch down, then spring up, pulling on the handlebars to lift the front wheel while at the same time pushing the feet hard back and up against the pedals to lift the back wheel. The aim is to get the bike level in midair and land the back wheel first, using the arms and legs as shock absorbers to control the landing.

Manuals are an important technique to master before progressing to jumps.

Bunny-hop are a great way to practise landing following a jump.

Front Endo

This is another exercise in weight shifting and balance. Roll slowly towards a kerb with pedals parallel to the ground. When the front wheel touches the kerb, straighten your arms and push the handlebars away from your body, while shifting your weight forward and bringing your legs up toward your body as the rear wheel lifts off the ground. Shift weight backward to hold the balance or gently lower the rear wheel.

Jumps

This is where work on wheelies, bunny-hops and manuals gets put into practice. Start on small jumps such as tabletops, so you get used to taking off and landing safely using the arms and legs as shock absorbers. Keep your body weight central on the bike and bend your legs and arms slightly as you approach the take-off. Maintain a firm grip on the bars and make sure the front wheel is pointing forward. Straighten your legs as you land. Make contact with the ground on both wheels or the rear wheel.

Front endo is an exercise in weight shifting, balance and control – skills that are essential to BMX success.

The big day

You are ready to enter your first race and feel excited and nervous at the prospect in equal measure. Keep calm: careful organisation and a positive attitude should ensure that your big day is memorable for all the right reasons.

Race day

You feel fit and ready to make your racing debut. If you have joined a cycling club or attended track training sessions, it's likely this will be a club event. But it pays to be well-organised even for the most informal race so you arrive at the start in the right frame of mind to do your best.

Pre-race Preparation

It's always best to pre-enter races well in advance to save money and reduce uncertainty. Race and entry form details can be found on the British Cycling and Cycling Time Trials websites.

Some events are designed to cater for novices by reducing entry formalities to a minimum; for others, British Cycling membership and a racing licence may be required (see pages 18–19). Make sure you meet the entry requirements for the event you are entering and take note of signing-on times for your event.

The Week Before

Sleep: make sure you have a good week of regular sleep, so you are fully rested on race day.

Bike: around a week before the race give your bike a thorough going-over, checking that the tyres are free of wear and cuts, the moving parts are properly adjusted and run smoothly and all bolts are tight. Doing this early in the week builds in enough time to visit a bike shop to replace parts should it be necessary.

Route: look up where the race is taking place and work out how long the journey will take. Add extra time to allow for unexpected traffic delays.

Weather: check the forecast as it will influence what you pack.

Kit Bag Checklist

Prepare a checklist of everything you need to take to the race:

Clothes: racing clothes and helmet, warm-up clothes, wet-weather gear and clothes to wear after the race.

Hygiene: take a towel, soap, shampoo and flannel as the minimum, plus a packet of wet wipes to clean oily hands or give yourself a rubdown if there are no showers.

Tools: take a puncture repair kit and tyre levers, pump, allen keys, multitool, chain tool, cross head and flat blade screwdrivers, adjustable spanner and chain lubricant. Mountain bikers are well advised to carry a sponge and bucket to clean the bike after the race.

Food and drink: bottles of sports drinks, water, energy bars, fruit and something substantial for after the race. A flask of hot soup, tea or coffee can be a godsend.

First-aid kit: carry plasters, antiseptic spray, painkillers and sun cream.

Paperwork: race startsheet, racing licence, directions from home to the race headquarters, safety pins for putting your race number on your jersey.

Extras: toilet paper and plastic bags, useful for dirty clothes.

The Day Before

Mountain bikers often arrive at races the day before as this allows them a chance to pre-ride the course. For other events, have a rest day and concentrate on getting your kit bag ready for the race. If you are making up sports drinks, have the ingredients and bottles out ready, so you can make them first thing on race day morning.

The Morning of the Race

Have a light breakfast and aim to arrive at the race with plenty of time in hand. The important thing is to have time to relax, stretch and go for a warm-up ride, so you are ready for the starting signal. When it goes, have fun and good luck.

Nothing can match the excitement and fun of a competitive race event.

Finding out more

Discovering more about bicycles and cycling will only increase your understanding and appreciation of both the machine and the sport. When you aren't out having fun on your bike, expand your knowledge and horizons by reading up on one of the world's most versatile activities.

The internet is awash with information on every aspect of cycling, from bike chic to the inner workings of bikes with three-speed hubs. Unfortunately, it is also a rich source of conflicting advice, which at best can baffle newcomers to the sport and at worst mislead them.

Training is a particular area of misinformation. Be wary of websites that offer training plans, because what works for one person may not work for someone else and may even do more harm than good. Coaching is not a one-off electronic transaction, it's an ongoing relationship between coach and athlete that can last for years.

The only reliable source of specific training advice is a coach with a UK Coaching Certificate (UKCC) – a nationally recognised qualification, who will offer guidance tailored to your needs.

Union Cycliste Internationale
uci.ch
Most of the information on the website of cycling's international governing body concerns elite category racing with calendars of events, rules, results and rankings for all branches of the sport.

British Cycling
britishcycling.org.uk
The website of the governing body for all branches of the sport except time trialling in Britain is a mine of information, covering everything from commuting and recreational riding to the Olympic athlete development programme. This is the site where you can find a club, a coach, a track, an event and much, much more.

Cycling Time Trials
cyclingtimetrials.org.uk
Everything you need to know about time trialling in Britain, including information specifically aimed at beginners, lists of clubs with contact numbers, age, categories, dates of races and details of the main competitions in the sport.

Reliable information and a qualified coach will put you on the path to cycling success.

CTC

ctc.org.uk
Britain's longest-established cycling
advocacy group isn't concerned with
competitive sport, but its website does
contain a lot of useful information for
newcomers to cycling and its members
organise rides all over the country.

Sustrans

sustrans.org.uk
The sustainable transport advocacy group
behind the 12,600-mile-long National

Cycle Network has a website with lots
of information about where to ride.

Cycle Maps Directory

cyclemaps.org.uk
A searchable database of cycle
routes produced by local councils
around the UK.

Index

Picture credits

The publishers would like to thank the following sources for their kind permission to reproduce the pictures in this book.

Action Images: /Carlos Barria/Reuters: 72-73; /Brandon Malone: 14, 15, 25, 47, 59; /Jacky Naegelen/Reuters: 17; /Phil Noble/Reuters: 65; /Jason O'Brien: 94; / Reuters: 12-13

Getty Images: 102; /AFP: 8-9, 52-53; /Martin Bernetti/AFP: 11, 40, 45, 85, 123; / Bloomberg: 107; /Central Press: 75; /Robert Cianflone: 18-19; /Carl de Souza/AFP: 121; /Stu Forster: 51, 104; /Daniel Garcia/AFP: 38-39, 49, 61, 89, 97; /Robert Laberge: 69; /Nicolas Lambert/AFP: 67; /Bryn Lennon: 71; /Popperfoto: 23; /Pascal Rondeau: 96; /Quinn Rooney: 86-87; /Axel Schmidt/AFP: 76, 103, 125; /Science & Society Picture Library: 22; /Bob Thomas: 95; /Phil Walter: 112; /Greg Wood/AFP: 43

Press Association Images: /All Action: 106; /ChinaFotoPress/Photocome: 57; /Zhang Duo/Landov: 113; /Christophe Ena/AP: 54-55; /John Giles: 6-7; /Paul Gilham: 20-21; /Andrew Milligan: 5; /Willis Parker/ABACA: 41; /Lucas Schifres/ABACA: 111; /Neal Simpson: 24

Every effort has been made to acknowledge correctly and contact the source and/ or copyright holder of each picture and Carlton Books Limited apologises for any unintentional errors or omissions that will be corrected in future editions of this book.